THE TEA PARTY Guide to Being a REAL AMERICAN

Arming Yourself against Godless Liberals, Dirty Socialists, & Sexy Ideas

ROLAND BOYLE

Copyright © 2011 by Roland Boyle
Cover and internal design © 2011 by Sourcebooks, Inc.
Cover design by Kirk DouPonce
Cover illustration by Milt Klingensmith

Sourcebooks and the colophon are registered trademarks of Sourcebooks, Inc.

Internal photos: courtesy of the Library of Congress, p. 1; © Alex Wong/Getty, p. 7; courtesy of Joey Weiser, p. 12; courtesy of the Ronald Reagan Presidential Library, p. 15; © Jim Watson/Getty, p. 17; courtesy of hankgilbert .com, p. 21; gun photos © AF archive/Alamy, © Antony Platt/Dreamstime.com, © Balefire9/Dreamstime.com, © Buriy/Dreamstime.com, © ewg3D/iStockphoto, © Horst Gossmann/Dreamstime.com, © Fotosergio/Dreamstime .com, © Goce Risteski/Dreamstime.com, © zlotysfor/iStockphoto, © Brand X Pictures/PunchStock, p.23–24; photo by Pfc. Christopher Grammer, p. 32; © Mark Wilson/Getty, p. 34; © Hiroko Masuike/Getty, p. 35; © John Moore/ Getty, p. 36; © David Becker/Getty, p. 37; © AFP/Getty, p. 38; photo by Gage Skidmore, p. 39; courtesy of the Library of Congress, p. 62; © Brendan Smialowski/Getty, p. 66; courtesy of the Library of Congress, p. 73; courtesy of the Library of Congress, p. 74; photo by Pete Souza, p. 80; courtesy of the Library of Congress, p. 83; photo by Justin Kendall, The Pitch, p. 87; photo by Hilary Richardson, p. 90; Tea Party protester illustration © Revilo, p. 91; Tea Party Protester illustration © Revilo, p. 92; Tea Party protester illustration © Revilo, p. 96; photo by Hilary Richardson, p. 100; courtesy of the United States Department of Justice, p. 118; courtesy of the Library of Congress, p. 119; courtesy of Harbin, p. 121; photo by Gage Skidmore, p. 142; photo by Nate Mandos, p. 149; photo by Fanny Bouton, p. 149; photo by Corporal Lynn Murillo, p. 150; photo by jonathanhstrauss, p. 150; photo by John VanderHaagen, p. 150; photo by Alan Light, p. 150; photo by Jerry Avenaim, p. 151; photo by David Shankbone, p. 152; photo by Ryan McFarland, p. 160; courtesy of the Library of Congress, p. 179; courtesy of the U.S. Department of Defense, p. 180; courtesy of the U.S. National Oceanic and Atmospheric Administration, p. 182; courtesy of Trish Adlesic, p. 185; courtesy by the Marine Photobank, p. 186; photo by Truejustice, p. 189; photo by Kjetil Bjørnsrud, p. 190; photo by Colin Chou, p. 191; photo by NASA, p. 192; courtesy of the Library of Congress, p. 193; © Mark Wilson/Getty, p. 194; photo by HKDP, p. 196; courtesy of the Library of Congress, p. 202; © Mark Wilson/Getty, p. 213; photo courtesy of the U.S. government, p. 215; © Mark Wilson/Getty, p. 215; © Washington Post/Getty, p. 215; © Tom Williams/Getty, p. 220; courtesy of the United State Sentate, p. 220; photo by Medineli, p. 223; photo by Christians United for Israel, p. 232; photo by Luke X. Martin, p. 237; photo by T&G Mardikes, p. 239

Published by Sourcebooks, Inc.
P.O. Box 4410, Naperville, Illinois 60567-4410
(630) 961-3900
Fax: (630) 961-2168
www.sourcebooks.com

Library of Congress Cataloging-in-Publication Data

Boyle, Roland.
  The Tea Party guide to being a real American : arming yourself against godless liberals, dirty socialists, and sexy ideas / Roland Boyle.
      p. cm.
  1. Political participation—United States—Humor. 2. Tea Party movement—Humor. 3. Tea Party Patriots—Humor. 4. Patriotism—United States—Humor. I. Title.
  PN6231.P6B64 2011
  818'.602—dc23

                              2011018812

          Printed and bound in the United States of America.
              VP 10 9 8 7 6 5 4 3 2 1

This book is dedicated to my parents,
Richard and Barbara Howard,
who endured my teen conspiracy theorizing,
taught me about history, writing, and love,
and still make America proud every day.

CONTENTS

ACKNOWLEDGMENTS

THE AUTHOR WOULD LIKE to acknowledge his inestimable debt to Adam Chromy of Artists & Artisans, literary manager extraordinaire, who told me to shut the hell up and write this book; and to Peter Lynch and Anne Hartman at Sourcebooks who rolled the dice on an unknown and didn't even yell "craps" when the first draft deserved it.

Thanks to Jill Lepore, whose splendid book, *The Whites of Their Eyes*, should be required reading in our oppressive, socialist public schools, and whose lecture at the Kansas City Public Library I attended and got her to sign my copy of said book, but where my favorite muffler was stolen, probably by liberals, because they think they can just take your stuff. Thanks a lot, liberals.

Thanks also to Coby Beck whose explanations of so-called climate science at *http://scienceblogs.com/illconsidered/about.php* are clear and accessible, although it is unclear why he hates America so much that he believes in global warming.

Big frackin' thanks to everybody who helped make the movie *Gasland* (especially Josh Fox, Debra Winger, and Trish Adlesic); and to the natural gas lobby, which has been funny, acrobatic, and free-spending in its attempts to discredit the film.

Thanks Dan Taylor, Emily Howard, and Ned Axthelm, for the state of jokes and jokes of states, and to Oliver Christianson, the greatest Revilo of all time.

And biggest, most unrepayable thanks to my family, Penny, Jonah, Emily, and Oliver, whose patience as I ignored them all to work on this book was that of Job, which is like a job, except it takes more time. I love you almost as much as I love America. Maybe as much. Maybe more. OK, more.

★★★

INTRODUCTION

THIS BOOK IS ON your side. It's not like all the others.

Other books are out to get you. You know the ones: novels that crush your spirit, sexy books with filthy sex in them, celebrity bios that make your life look like homemade caca by comparison. Other books are the work of the devil.

At the very least, they're selling something: diet plans, new age relationship advice, and—worst of all—ideas. Other books spread ideas like deadly mold spores into the bathroom of your mind, mucking up the clean white tile of your thoughts and staining the grout of your morals, because the exhaust fan of your judgment is, well, exhausted.

Yet judge we must. There's so much wrongness (see Chapter 4)! So much to protest (see Chapter 5)! So many Tea Party parties, so little gun control (see Chapter 2)! This book will help you make the right judgments, find the right parties, and right the right wrongs. It will confirm you as a Real American, which means being right, right, right.

America is always right. It's always had the right answers when history asked the big questions, such as: *What are you doing with that tea?* (1773). *How far will you go to preserve the Union?* (1861–1865). *How do you spot communists?* (1950s/'60s). *Bin Laden was living in a mansion in the middle of a Pakistani suburb, and it took ten years to find him?* (2011).

This book, like America, has the answers. Good thing, too, as we are now faced with the *most important question ever* in the history of mankind. That's because all people in the history of mankind believe they are the most important people in the history of mankind. The question is simple:

How can we tell who the Real Americans are?

Now, you may be thinking, "If you have to ask, you're not one, son." That's a good start, because suspicion and superiority are two of the legs of the table that is America. The other two legs, of course, are the flag and also the flag, which is so important that it's two. Sitting on that table is a gleaming set of the kind of china that doesn't want to see your children in athletic jerseys and pajama pants at dinnertime. And all the plates, forks, and napkin rings represent principles of democracy, but this is getting complicated.

For the most important question ever, what we need is a simple answer. The truth is always simple. It doesn't tolerate things like "nuance" or "interpretation." The truth is as dumb as a box of hammers, and it's only with these hammers that we can beat the right answer to this question and other pesky questions into people's heads. Consider this book your own hammer collection. Especially if you bought it in hardback.

The answer it pounds in isn't earth-shattering: you already know it, deep in your heart. We've all known it since we were Real Little Americans.

Back then, if we asked questions about America, adults would give us the right answers, because they had clean thought tiles and strong moral grout. *America is good*, they'd say. *America is God's country*, they'd preach. *America is infallible like Catholics think the Pope is, but they're wrong, because the Catholic church is the Great Whore of Babylon*, they'd pant—*and that's why Kennedy was shot and it all goes back to the Freemasons and the Illuminati and a worldwide communist conspiracy, which has turned our culture into a cesspool and fluoridated our water*, they'd spit, with a wild gleam in their eyes. So we loved America, feared communism, and drank Kool-Aid instead of water.

But as we grew older, godless liberals ruined everything, secretly changing the Kool-Aid flavor from right to wrong. These everything-ruiners taught us that America has flaws and bad countries are good and fluoride prevents cavities, plus a lot of science thingies. We were taught evolution (refuted in Chapters 4 and 11), environmentalism (chopped down in Chapter 10), and sex (not quite repressed in Chapter 7) education.

Wait, don't flip to Chapter 7 just because it's got sex in it! Hey, come back!

See what's happened to America? Because everything's been ruined, you're now reading Chapter 7 instead of this introduction. You're missing the main point, which is that this book, in addition to being a box of hammers, is also a roadmap to the Real America. Go ahead, try to unfold it and then fold it back up. Pretty hard, huh?

This book points you down the right road and hammers out the Tea Party platform, which, like the fabled table of America, is built on legs of important principles (lower taxes! bigger guns!) and the flag. But let's add a pop-out fifth leg: outrage. It's the wrong length, because it was added in a blind fury, so it makes things uneven and wobbly, the same way Tea Party outrage has shaken up America.

That's where this book really comes in handy: just place it under that leg and the Tea Party platform stands sturdy and strong in its resolve, unshakable in its faith that the best days for all Real Americans are ahead of us, or at least off to the side, maybe down in a ditch, but still visible from the platform. Stay on that platform. If you wander off of it, use this roadmap to find your way back.

And if anyone tries to stop you, teabag 'em.

CHAPTER ONE

★★★

AMERICA IS GOOD.
EVERYTHING ELSE IS BAD.

LOOK AT THIS PICTURE of the original Boston Tea Party by Nathaniel Currier, of Currier & Ives, who also designed your parents' or grandparents' dinnerware, which they got cheap back in the 1950s or early '60s when everything was good. You may remember eating meatloaf off of an image of a horse-drawn sleigh and arranging meatloaf crumbs behind the

Boston Tea Party!

horse, causing your sister to laugh at this classic poop joke. Then you got slapped upside the head for that. Even meatloaf and getting slapped were good back then.

But back to the picture. This book knows what you're thinking. You're thinking, "Hey, why does Currier's iconic 1846 lithograph of this 1773 event show Mohawk Indians dumping the tea into the harbor? Who invited *them* to the party? And why are all those Bostonians just standing there holding their hats, waiting for a three-cornered handout?"

Well, think no more. Let this book be your thought-substitute, as it explains that Currier took artistic liberties with history. He used a minor anecdote about a few protesters in Mohawk garb and turned it into what appears to be a tribal takeover of the whole event. And those colonists want reform, not handouts. They're taking their hats off and cheering, letting their periwigs down. They're partying. They're starting a revolution. If Currier were alive today, he could paint the same thing, only with beer and handguns instead of tea and hats.

As today's Tea Party reminds us again and again, America began as a tax revolt. This, with the right to bear arms and the blessing of Jesus Christ, our Lord and Savior Whether You Like It or Not, is the basis of our essential goodness.

XENOPHOBES ABROAD

Other countries are bad. Oh, Canada has some nice people tramping around the woods with guns, and Mexico does love it some Jesus, and New Zealand has no capital-gains tax.

Even Russia has its good points, such as vodka. But nobody else has America's perfect storm of goodness, and everybody else knows it. If you travel the world (which this book does NOT recommend) the first thing you notice is how other countries constantly express their inferiority, usually in a foreign language. That's right—they're so ashamed of not being America, they won't even admit it in Real Words.

This should make us feel sorry for them, but we're Americans. We go straight to feeling righteously indignant. Then we start shooting to assert our essential goodness in other countries and to get them to be good like us—and fortunately there are plenty of weapons to help us do that. That's pretty much the foreign policy that led to the Iraq war.

But what if you're in a country where they won't let you drive around in a tank or shoot people on sight? Or maybe you're just weakened by the diarrhea that other cultures inflict on us out of jealousy. Whatever the reason for your momentary inability to work up some good old-fashioned American self-righteousness, you'll need to fake it. This requires a rudimentary understanding of the "words" that un-Americans around you are "saying." Let's deal with that theoretical diarrhea of yours, using this simple translation table to "listen" and then respond as a Real American.

If this un-American…	says this…	it means this…	so you say this:
Canadian	"Trés bon free health care, eh?"	"Yo, socialism!"	"I'd prefer a market-based solution. Also, do you have any more toilet paper?"
Mexican	"¿Cerveza?"	"Don't drink the water, yo!"	"I'll drink whatever damn thing I want oh God these abdominal cramps please Lord just kill me and kill these un-Americans before they cross our borders."
Russian	"Do svidaniya!"	"You're in the wrong line. This is the line for prison vodka. The line for toilet paper starts at the other end of the Gulag."	"This prison vodka is better than I'd expect, given that you made it from turnips and fermented socks, but we Americans have a proud history of freedom and you're cramping my style. Also, my abdomen."

If this un-American...	says this...	it means this...	so you say this:
New Zealander	"Care to wash down that Imodium with a glass of the national beverage?"	"Kiwis have to drink Sauvignon Blanc 24/7 to endure not being Americans."	"Yes, Mr. Frodo, if it will help with my electrolyte balance."
Liberal Democrat[1]	"Let's work together to solve problems for the American people."	"Support the new Tushy Tax Program to wipe out diarrhea in our lifetime."	"No."

As the translation table shows: it all comes back to taxes. The same issue that led to the original Tea Party is the issue that unites the Tea Party of today. To understand this connection, to draw a direct line between America's founding fathers and the founding mother and father (Sarah Palin and Glenn Beck) of today's Real America, you'll need a brief crash course in the events that took place between then and now.

---

1 *You may think: wait—aren't liberal Democrats Americans, too? Technically, yes, although we'd need to check their birth certificates to be sure, and liberals won't show you their birth certificates, and if they do, it's not a real birth certificate, because liberals are actually un-American, so to answer your question: Technically, no.*

HISTORY: ONE THING AFTER ANOTHER, AND THEN THAT ONE THING AGAIN

Those who do not learn from history are doomed to read clichés about it. But, as always, it's way simpler to understand than fancy academics and so-called experts would have us believe. If you've seen one little snippet of history, you've seen it all, because it repeats itself. For example, this handy timeline below shows the course America has taken since God created it in His image and gave it dominion over all other nations.

Tax revolt	God creates America	Jesus writes Constitution	Republicans free the slaves	Obama elected	Middle-class tax cut	Tax revolt

Is that really all there is to American history? No. This great country has a rich heritage, and there's no way to cram it all into something as brief and ignorance-based as this book. There's the Louisiana Purchase, for example, when Thomas Jefferson bought a whole state, complete with Superdome. There's the Lewis and Clark expedition to explore the jazz clubs and Creole restaurants of that great state. There's, like, Yalta? The details aren't important, because all these things are just going to happen again. In fact, we've already spent millions rediscovering Louisiana after it disappeared under the Gulf of Mexico in 2005. We've probably had another Yalta, too, but they kept it a secret, the same way they did the real facts of Kennedy's assassination and Area 51. The point about history is that it's cyclical, which means that once you learn how to ride it (or rewrite it), you never forget how.

Most Americans have forgotten a lot of their proud history. Why? Because it's boring. Who can remember all the wars and treaties and Hawley-Smoot tariffs of yesteryear, much less draw lessons from them? Well, maybe Doris Kearns Goodwin can.

America is good.
Goodwin is bad.

You know this smarty-pants lady. She's the historian who's always showing up on talk shows to discuss the historical implications of current events. She's a Harvard Ph.D. and had a White House fellowship and knows everything there is to know about Abraham Lincoln, Eleanor Roosevelt, and Lyndon Johnson. She think she all that.

This book almost caught up with Doris Kearns Goodwin recently, and learned of her sinister plot to educate Americans about history, even though we don't like it. Here's an excerpt from the interview this book failed to have with her.

★ **TEA PARTY GUIDE:** Think you're pretty smart there, don't you, with your "facts" and your three names and your Woodrow Wilson Fellowship and so forth?

★ **Doris Kearns Goodwin:** Well, I just try to bring the past to life, by—

★ **TPG:** Oh, so you're saying the past is dead?

★ **DKG:** Uh…

★ **TPG:** And you believe you can resurrect it? The way Jesus did with Lazarus?

★ **DKG:** Well, it's not quite like that—

★ **TPG:** Ah-ha! So you're NOT Jesus!

★ **DKG:** Of course not. I'm just an American historian—

★ **TPG:** You call yourself an American?!

★ **DKG:** Yes. I was born in Brooklyn—

★ **TPG:** Ah-ha! A New Yorker! A member of the liberal elite!

★ **DKG:** Oh, I don't think so. I've worked as a sports journalist—

★ **TPG:** That's right. Isn't it true that you were the first female reporter—

★ **DKG:**—to enter the Boston Red Sox locker room? Yes, I was.

★ **TPG:** You seem anxious to talk about that.

★ **DKG:** Well, it was very exciting. Breaking the gender barrier. Getting the scoop. Seeing Jim Rice naked.

★ **TPG:** Did you see Wade Boggs naked as well?

★ **DKG:** I didn't see him as well as I did Jim Rice. [sighs]

★ **TPG:** So, why Boston? Why Massachusetts? Why not a red state? You could have covered the Texas Rangers, or the Arizona Wetbacks—

★ **DKG:** Massachusetts is home. I live in Concord.

★ **TPG:** Ah-ha! A member of the liberal elite with mandatory state health care!

★ **DKG:** Uh…

★ **TPG:** And gay marriage!

★ **DKG:** Is this imaginary interview almost over?

★ **TPG:** It was over before it began.

★ **DKG:** Thank goodness.

★ **TPG:** When you thank goodness, you're thanking America. America is good, in case you hadn't noticed!

★ **DKG:** …

★ **TPG:** And everything else is bad!

★ **DKG:** Everything?

★ **TPG:** Yes, including you. Your name should be Doris Kearns Badwin.

★ **DKG:** Good one.

★ **TPG:** No, Badwin.

★ **DKG:** I think we're done here.

Then she walked out of the non-interview, without even answering a parting question about her Woodrow Wilson Fellowship, which tells you all you need to know about Doris Kearns Goodwin. Woodrow Wilson?! Glenn Beck HATES that guy!

IRS AGENTS WERE WILSON'S BITCHES

All Real Americans should hate Woodrow Wilson, the father of the income tax. By "father," of course, we mean that he wasn't there when it was born. That makes William Howard Taft the "mother of the income tax," which may be why he looked pregnant and bloated much of the time. Yes, it was Taft, not Wilson, who hustled America with the income tax. Wilson just reaped the cash as if he were the Internal Revenue Service's pimp. Even his name sounds pimpesque. You can practically hear IRS agents whining, "Woodrow, I busted a heel on the curb," and then he slaps them and gets in a big fight with Prussia.

But as pimps go, Wilson wasn't too muthafuggin' bad. Instead of spending all that tax money on fancy cars or broad-brimmed hats or social programs, he used it to replace lost tariff revenue. Wilson lowered tariffs, see, because he was actually a free-market-lovin' conservative, not a big-government liberal. He also enjoyed forcing democracy on other countries (straight out of the right-wing playbook), got America into war, and appointed a Supreme Court Justice who later opposed every one of FDR's New Deal programs. So we should actually love Woodrow Wilson, except that we've been told by our parental Tea Party authorities to hate him. So hatred it is!

The misunderstanding of Wilson is the only thing Glenn Beck ever got wrong.[2] Everything else he says is true.[3] His grasp of history is unimpeachable.[4] And as he generously shares[5] it in his brilliant lectures[6], we receive the gift of America's enduring legacy.[7] True, much of this history has been debunked by so-called scholars, and Beck's insights are cribbed from W. Cleon Skousen, the Mormon conspiracy theorist and founding-fathers fetishist who famously frittered away his family fortune on a pair of George Washington's dentures and had his own teeth pulled in order to wear them, only to find out that they were not dentures at all, but a matched wooden paddle-ball set. Skousen nearly choked to death on the rubber balls before realizing his mistake.

---

2 *Except other statements made between 1964 and today's date (—ed.)*

3 *Unless fact-checked (which I do, even if no one else does. —ed.)*

4 *Where "unimpeachable" means "fuzzy" (Get it straight, Boyle. —ed.)*

5 *Read "obsessively foists" (Good thing you have an editor, Boyle! —ed.)*

6 *A.k.a. "mendacious, tear-soaked screeds" (Figure it out, Boyle! —ed.)*

7 *And by "receive the gift of America's enduring legacy" we mean "endure the rhetorical equivalent of fingernails screeching across a chalkboard filled with incomprehensible diagrams and misspellings" (Getting the idea, Boyle? —ed.)*

Skousen: choked
on balls.

This yammering Pappy Yokum's vision of America as a three-headed eagle perched precariously between the perils of anarchy and tyranny gave Beck his idea for "the tripartite Mormon theocracy that will save America from the evil of Progressivism," although the idea to represent this trinity as a three-headed giraffe perched precariously on top of a bus stop shelter came not from Skousen, but, Beck admits, "from smoking a little too much weed in my twenties."

But who among us hasn't gotten high and put up a three-headed giraffe bus stop shelter to represent a Mormon triumvirate? That's the secret of Tea Party populism: no matter what crazy stunt you've pulled—any DUI or drug-addled act of narcissism, any preposterous distortion or outright lie you've spread, any state funding you've slashed for unwed mothers while accepting a governor's salary and benefits that provide for your pregnant teenage daughter's pre-natal care, any assault you may have committed against the sensibilities of a community or a nation—your Tea Party leaders have already done it.

BUT WAIT, THIS BOOK DIGRESSES

We'll get to Sarah and Glenn later. For now, we're just laying the groundwork, swerving hither and yon to suggest the redundancy and incoherent magnitude of history, establishing links between the Tea Party of yore and the Tea Party of yours. This amazingly tenuous connection to the early colonists and their struggle against the yoke of tyranny is a big part of Teabagger culture. We've traded in our handbills and powdered wigs for protest signs and baldness (except for those of us into cosplay involving wigs, buckledy shoes, and corsets—a favorite getup of GOP lobbyist and Tea Party money-launderer Dick Armey), but we carry on the tradition of dissent.

The first modern Tea Party protest, four days after Obama's unconstitutional inauguration, targeted New York's "obesity tax" on sodas and sugary juice drinks as patriotic "New Porkers" reclaimed our revolutionary roots, yanked them out of the ground, and shook them in the face of government oppression. It's not all about taxes, though. Let's examine other remarkable similarities that connect Tea Party patriots across the centuries.

Tea Party of Yore	Tea Party of Yours
Not a political party, but a single revolt	Not a political party, but fond of one
Fighters in the war for independence	Fighters against the "War on Christmas"
Many wore three-cornered hats	Many have pointy heads
Led by Samuel Adams	Influenced by beer
Destroyed British tea by dumping it in Boston Harbor	Destroy Krispy Kremes by dunking and eating them
Stood on principle	Shout on Fox News
Rallied against the authority of the "red coats"	Rally with the author of "The Christmas Sweater"

Note that two of the parallels there involve Christmas. That's because our founding fathers were Christian, and *that's* because Jesus was one of them. His disciples (Matthew, Mark, Luke, John Adams, James Madison, St. Thomas Jefferson, etc.), built into the very foundation of this great country the Christian virtues of free markets, individual liberty, and the right to bear arms.

MORE ON THAT RIGHT TO BEAR ARMS IN A MINUTE, MAN

Since history repeats itself, all those Christian virtues got re-established under the second coming of Christ, Ronald Reagan. True, some naysayers naysay that we're still waiting for the second coming, that Jesus will descend from heaven to land atop the rotunda of the Capitol and blast it like those aliens did in *Independence Day*. But for those of us who witnessed the Reagan Miracle of the 1980s, in which lepers were healed and Nicaraguan contras funded through a "peace that passeth understanding" with Iran, the divinity of Reagan is as self-evident as the truths held in the Declaration of Independence (John 3:16). The Gipper remains, for Teabaggers, a conservative savior who brought us out of the malaise of the Carter years, single-handedly defeated communism, was crucified by the liberal media, and then was resurrected by every subsequent Republican who has ever run for office. We all ride Reagan's coattails into the future, where presumably there will be some sort of third coming.

The Gipper in bailout crash-pants.

But as Real Americans, it is our right to worship Reagan out of one side of our mouths as we spit on his grave out of the other. Reagan couldn't win the GOP nomination today—not because he's dead (that didn't stop McCain in 2008, after all), but because he was too liberal. Reagan raised taxes in 1982, 1983, and 1984. He vastly expanded the IRS to collect those taxes. He proposed amnesty for illegals! He spent hundreds of billions to bail out the savings and loan industry AND Chrysler! If he were president today, we'd label him a socialist. Obviously he wouldn't listen, because, as noted, he's dead—as all socialists should be. The next national messiah had better be able to beat the Gip at his own conservative game.

See why America is good? We don't care if we contradict ourselves. And we don't depend on "facts" for our understanding of history. If we did, we'd feel bad about things like slavery, genocidal campaigns against native tribes, the destruction of the environment, the exploitation of labor by moneyed interests, and nearly every moment from 2001 through 2008. But we don't even think about these things. Why? Because America's goodness doesn't need to be examined or explained. It's a feeling. We feel good about the founding fathers even though they had slaves. We affectionately call Andrew Jackson "Ol' Hickory" instead of "Ol' Ethnic Cleanser of Native America." We love Lincoln even though he was ugly. We revere Martin Luther King, Jr. despite his penchant for social justice. And we feel all warm and squishy about Reagan, because he made us feel proud of the country his policies nearly ruined. When he said, "Mr. Gorbachev, tear down this wall," he raised goosebumps as well as taxes, and made us remember that we were the boss of Russia and Germany and all those other loser nations. He reminded us of the Founders, because he was almost as old as one. He was our grandpa, affable and clueless and utterly adorable.

Not even Saudi-lovin' George Bush, Sr., intern-bangin' Bill Clinton, or corporation-blowin' George Bush, Jr., could dismantle Reagan's legacy of good. Not even Obama can do it, because, like everyone else, he fell in love with Nancy Reagan.

Nancy Reagan, about to get Frenched by a Kenyan.

The Gipper lives on as a national fantasy that grandpa's gonna shuffle in with his fusty old hand tools and fix our broken republic. Close your eyes and recall Reagan's smiling, bobble-headed, "Well…" as he tried to remember why he was standing in front of the press corps. Feel that? You're taking a warm bath in Real American goodness.

While you're in that bath, the phone rings, and it's the future calling. It asks, "What's the Tea Party doing to preserve Real American values for me?" Now you know. Having read this chapter, you can explain to the future that yesterday's

Tea Party and today's are one and the same, separated only by a bunch of recurring history. You can show the future how today's Real Americans are working furiously to make sure that tomorrow's Real Americans enjoy the same goodness that yesterday's Real Americans did. How? By being furious, and by defending and protecting the Constitution from its enemies, both foreign and domestic—which covers both Barack Hussein Obama and Nancy Satan Pelosi.

If the future asks, "But what about the Second Amendment, which that socialist Obama (with fascist attorney general Eric Holder) is ruining, stealing our guns and kissing white women and spending taxpayer money on Secret Service protection from good old-fashioned assassination attempts?" you can say, "Thanks for the segue to the next chapter of *The Tea Party Guide*, where we'll explore a deep connection between the original Tea Party and today's unoriginal one: the packing of the heat." If namby-pamby liberals don't like that, they can go back to Jolly Olde England, where possession of a handgun might just land them in "gaol." (And they say *we* can't spell!)

Kaboom! America's goodness proven. Lock, load, and read on.

CHAPTER TWO

THE GUNSTITUTION OF THE UNITED STATES

MUCH HAS BEEN MADE in the media of the Tea Party's love of guns. At every rally, photographers salivate as they capture heroic images of Real Americans with rifles slung over their shoulders or handguns jammed into thigh holsters. The liberal media then buys these images, using Photoshop to remove the heroism and add craziness. But will they allow this book to reprint their precious photographs without having to pay an arm and a thigh-holstered leg? No. They wouldn't even return this book's phone calls. Those media jackals should all be shot. They're technically protected by the First Amendment, so be sure to use amendment-piercing ammo.

When Jesus and his founding disciples wrote the Bill of Rights (John 3:16), they made your freedom to shoot stuff second only to your freedom of religion, speech, the press, assembly, and one other thing this book can never remember. Some nerdish stickler might say that puts your firearms freedom in sixth place, but remember that this freedom has its own entire amendment. Those first freedoms have to split one amendment five ways, like five guys who have only enough money for one pizza. The Second Amendment gets a whole pizza to itself, which is fair, because it went out and killed its own pepperoni in the wild. You gotta respect that. Any amendment that can make it all the way to number two (with a bullet!) in the Constitution is good enough for Chapter 2 of *The Tea Party Guide*.

THE ACTUAL WORDS OF THE ACTUAL GUYS WHO ACTUALLY WROTE THE ACTUAL THING

Now, some persnickety liberals insist that the so-called "language" of the Second Amendment limits the right to bear arms to a "well regulated militia." Sit back while this book takes aim and fills that canard full of holes. (A "canard," by the way, is a duck—which is what those liberals had better do. But it also means a stupid thing that people say right before they try to steal your guns.)

Here's how your freedom looks in the original copy of the Constitution, which apparently has an action figure of Thomas Jefferson glued to it:

Let's examine each part of this amendment carefully. The first word is "Awell." That's an eighteenth-century contraction of the phrase, "Ah, well, let's just leave that militia alone." "Awell" modifies the word "regulated." So, what kind of regulation were the founders talking about? The kind where you just leave that militia alone. That's what's "necessary to the security of a free State," and that's why "the right of the People to keep and bear arms shall not be infringed." Period.

Some "scholars" may dispute this explanation, claiming that the language refers to "a militia" that is to be "well regulated." To do this, they move "a" next to "militia," a typical sleight-of-word trick that intellectuals will pull if you don't watch them like a hawk. So if some egghead tries that, you can say, "Oh, so you just move words around to make stuff mean whatever you want? Interesting. I myself prefer THE WAY THE FOUNDING FATHERS WROTE IT." Practice this until you can speak in all capital letters. If necessary, pull a gun as you say it. Scholars hate that.

Or, counter with your own crazy interpretation. Insist that "well regulated" actually means "regulated through the use of a well," and that wells were often used for weapons storage by eighteenth-century militias, a practice that Iraqi villagers still employ in films such as *Three Kings* (1999), David O. Russell's darkly comic Gulf War film starring George Clooney, Mark Wahlberg, and Ice Cube. By the time you're finished reviewing the film and pointing out that Spike Jonze also starred in it (and that his own films include *Being John Malkovich* and *Where the Wild Things Are*) your scholarly opponent will usually have forgotten what you were arguing about in the first place. If not, simply segue from *Where the Wild Things Are* to *The Wild Bunch* and pull a gun.

In fact, why go through the charade of debating the Second Amendment at all? Being a Real American is not about talk. The original Tea Party didn't need words, and neither do we. We're about action. We're about revolution. We're about to pull guns at any moment, so cut to the chase. Pull the gun for starters, instead of as a last resort. You'll save time, freedom, and maybe even lives…well, probably not lives.

TICKETS TO THE GUN SHOW

You may be wondering what kind of gun you should pull. If you're new to the Tea Party and have not yet amassed a huge cache of weapons, you're infringing upon your own right to keep and bear arms. You could get shot for that. You'd better move fast, stock up, and get familiar with your friendly persuaders. Here's everything you need to know about a few basic weapon types.

Gun type:	Examples:	Nicknames:	Best uses:
.22 caliber ladystinger		J. Walther Reed	botched assassinations
.38 caliber revolver		Mr. Smith, "teach 'em a Wesson"	protection from big government
9 mm handgun		My Plastic Playmate, Lil' Glocky	street cred, tamping down paranoia
.44 magnum brain splatterer		Make-My-Day-O	compensation for a small penis
bazooka		no nicknames cuz it's already fun to say	compensation for a *really* small penis
shotgun		Fudd	canard hunting
muzzleloader		Johnny Wad, Swabby McSwabbington	piracy, Civil War re-enactments

Gun type:	Examples:	Nicknames:	Best uses:
M-16		Charlton, Fragarooni, Ol' Ammo-jammer	Vietnam flashback re-enactments
Kalashnikov AK-47		Trusty Russkie, Osama-rama-ding-dong	selling to anti-American insurgents
handheld surface-to-air missile launcher		Over-the-Shoulder Eric-Holder-Smolderer	blowin' crap up

But don't just think you can roll into your corner Walmart and load up the basket on your Amigo with these bare necessities. No siree. Thanks to the liberals and other un-Americans, the infringement of your right to keep and bear arms has reached a tipping point that makes buying even a dinky little ladystinger nearly impossible. You can also forget about ammo—it's all been bought by panicked gun owners preparing for all-out war against the government. Even if your friendly firearms retailer has the ammo you need, most states won't let them put it in the same area of the store as the guns. It's like buying a car with no gas in it, so you have to push it down the street to a filling station—except nobody asks about your criminal record when you buy a car.

Yep, believe it or not, to exercise your God-given right to sting ladies or blast black helicopters out of the sky, you have to register your guns with the government. You can't buy a gun until Big Brother does a "background check," which tells him everything about you, including where to find you when he comes to take the gun back after you buy it.

Is your blood boiling yet? Well, it should be. (If you have a gun handy, you can easily check by shooting yourself to see if steam comes out.) Since 1934, when Congress regulated the sale of machine guns, the government has been steadily whittling away at the Second Amendment. That's why some gun-rights advocates have attempted to ban whittling knives—an unpopular idea among most weapons enthusiasts.

Granted, the 1994 ban on assault weapons was allowed to expire in 2004, which is sort of the opposite of whittling away. The expiration of this ban allows the flow of military-grade weaponry into civilian hands without anyone paying much attention—the kind of militia-regulating our founding gun-nuts had in mind. Also bucking the trend, a 2008 Supreme Court decision took the background check away from the federal government and left the states in control, which means that if you find your state's gun control policy too restrictive, you can blow up your house and move somewhere else.

This raises a big question: In *Call of Duty: Black Ops*, how do you adjust for the inaccuracy of those machine pistols in Sharp Shooter mode? Wait, that's not it (but if you have an answer, please let this book know). The question is, where are the best places for us Real Americans and our firearms to live without state and local governments getting all up in our business, busting us, and making us serve a really long sentence?

A REALLY LONG SENTENCE

The Tea Party Guide is here to answer that question and help you make your last stand—but remember, wherever you set up your cache and bunker, there's no guarantee of freedom in this embattled nation, because as we saw at Waco in 1993, even a shoot-'em-all-and-let-God-sort-'em-out state like Texas can be overrun by federal agents hell-bent on the infringement of a religious cult's right to keep and bear automatic arms, armor-piercing bullets, silencers, hand grenades, and .50 caliber rifles—which is obviously the kind of stuff Jesus would stockpile—so naturally a cult leader who claimed to be the second coming of Christ would, too, especially if he had to defend himself against the ATF and FBI, who were not only out to take his guns but trying to stop him from having sex with ten-year-old girls even though God told him to do it.

Whew, that sentence makes this book want to lie down. But no! It will not rest until it lets you know where the Second Amendment is treated with the reverence and selective literalism it deserves. And conversely, this book wants you to know where you *shouldn't* go: places where this Amendment has been spat upon by liberals, shat upon by lawmakers, and probably shot upon, too, with weapons confiscated by officials whose secret agenda is to render this country an easy mark for takeover by fascist socialist pacifist dictators.

How was this secret agenda uncovered? *The Tea Party Guide* scoured the USA for the best Tea Party activities—which of course feature guns aplenty (you'll see those state-by-state surveys in later chapters)—and, along the way, discovered some surprising things about gun laws in the fifty states. There's good news, and there's pants-soilingly terrifying bad news. Let's get the bad news over with first.

STATES THAT TREAT THE SECOND AMENDMENT LIKE NUMBER TWO

You don't even want to visit these five states, much less set up your Ruby Ridge Memorial Machine Shop and Gun Lair in them. The restrictions they place on your pursuit of trigger happiness are like a slap in the face of the Founding Fathers, who would ordinarily respond by taking ten paces, turning, and firing, but must now look to you to defend their honor. Naturally, you would do this, but when you reach for your gun, you'll come up with a handful of regulations instead.

NEW YORK

Sure, go ahead, live here. New York invented gun control and turned it into a racket, using your tax money to buy back your guns and sell them to urban gangs who rob and kill you—and that's one of their better programs. Wait until they strip-search you and dump you naked on 42nd Street, not that anyone there will notice. Wait until you wake up dead in front of that Ground Zero mosque, with terrorists and congressmen prying your gun from your cold, Charlton-Hestonesque hands. Then maybe you'll heed this book.

HAWAII

The last state to be ratified is among the first in ratting out gun buyers, with its waiting period for permits, mental health requirements, and FBI fingerprinting. County police chiefs can deny your permit for any reason, including, "Sorry, dude, gotta catch some waves." The list of banned weapons is as long as a Hawaiian surname and even harder to figure out. Carrying a loaded firearm—even in the privacy of your own panel van—is a class-A felony. No wonder the Japanese snuck up on these guys. Who was there to stop 'em? No Real American in his right mind would live here.

ILLINOIS

Big problem here: there's no state preemption of local firearm laws. So, say you're a hard-workin' Illinois farmer/Tea Partier drivin' a truckload of freshly harvested Glocks from Kankakee to a farmer's market/rally in Chicago. You're safer now than you were before 2010, when the Supreme Court struck down Chicago's ban on handguns. But then Rahm Emanuel's cronies slapped up a new law the very next month, forcing you to wait forever for a permit and requiring you to pass a safety training course. The point is, this is no place to be a Glock farmer.

MINNESOTA

As you'd expect, this blue state has some of the dumbest gun control laws on the books, including a thirty-day waiting period for a permit. Here's all you need to know: state law preempts local weapons ordinances, *except for the discharge of those weapons*. In other words: you can have a gun, you just can't fire it. So what if the state says you can carry a nuclear-pulse plasma blaster? If every podunk town in Minnesota decides that you can't kill aliens with it, where's the fun?

CALIFORNIA

No assault weapons. Thumbprint and state ID required to buy ammunition. And now they're going for microstamping technology that ties spent ammo to the gun that fired it. What's next, GPS implants in the brains of gun owners to track our whereabouts? Don't bother, because California, here we don't come.

STATES THAT WELCOME GUNS WITH OPEN ARMS AND SUCKING CHEST WOUNDS

The following are five great places to keep and bear arms—also to buy, sell, smuggle, hoard, carry, show off, threateningly brandish, fire, and fire some more. Make no mistake, Real Americans: there is a target on the back of every gun, and the forces of tyranny are aiming at it. Our weapons will survive only if we all band together in places where there's still a love of shootin' stuff up.

TEXAS

They have the "Castle Doctrine" here, which means if you're in your house and someone breaks in, you can kill 'em with impunity. (Be sure to name your gun "Impunity.") Combine that with a recent law that allows RV drivers to carry concealed weapons without a permit, and you can shoot "an intruder" just for parking too close to your mobile home. Automatic weapons? (Check!) Sawed-off shotguns? (Check!) Silencers? (!) They didn't adopt the motto, "Don't mess with Texas" for nothing.

MONTANA

Montanans believe that anybody can have a gun—and they mean *anybody*. Criminal record? Have a gun. Escaping from a mental institution? Better take a gun with you. Small child? Here, play with this gun. Local governments do have some jurisdiction here and there, but for the most part, the state insists that you carry a gun, fire it a lot, and keep a bunch more of them in that cabin in the woods where you write your manifestos.

KENTUCKY

To be clear, Kentucky does regulate firearms, but it's so crazy here, the regulations are really wacky and nobody enforces them. True, you have to be a resident of the state for six months to apply for a permit—but nobody cares if you have a permit. You can carry a gun in your glove compartment, but not in the center console of your car. You can drive that gun onto school property as long as you don't wave it at anybody— but that only applies to Kentucky permit-holders; if your gun is licensed in another state, go ahead, wave it around. Best of all, the state cannot seize your weapons in the event of a disaster or emergency. Just being in Kentucky qualifies as a disaster or emergency, so they can't touch you. (NOTE: If you're their cousin, they probably will touch you.)

NEVADA

An open-carry state with no registration required. Nice. If you qualify to carry a revolver (by winning a game of craps), you can carry ANY revolver. This probably includes machine guns with roulette-wheel magazines. What gets shot in Vegas stays shot in Vegas—also in Reno, where you can kill a man just to watch him die.

VERMONT

Gun rights advocates have been known to use Vermont's gun laws (a one-page government pamphlet) as bathroom inspiration for pleasuring themselves. Then they go out and shoot maple trees and drink syrup straight from the tap. It's paradise here, if you don't count the brutal winters and that socialist senator, Bernie Sanders. The famed "Vermont Carry" (concealed or open, no permit required) is a touchstone for Real Americans who think that if everyone carried guns all the time, we'd all be safer, look cooler, and could pursue happiness until it lay bloody and vanquished at our feet.

MORE ON THE STATE OF THE STATES

Utah and Wyoming are good, too. You're probably thinking, what about Alaska and Arizona? Don't they make Vermont look like a police state? Wouldn't Arizona kick Kentucky's confused ass? Isn't Alaska what Montana whines about wanting to be when it sits around drinking with Idaho? Yes, that's all true. Move to Arizona. But there's a reason you should think twice before moving to Alaska, and its name is Sarah Palin.

Mama Grizzly takes aim at coherent language.

Don't get this book wrong—it loves it some Sarah. But let's not kid ourselves. She didn't do her home state any favors by pointing out its proximity to Russia. Russia didn't even know this before she opened her big yap. All their maps got used for toilet paper back in the 1970s and 1980s, so today's Russkies had no idea that Alaska was just a hop and skip across the Bering Strait. Now Putin knows where we are, and our Queen Mama Grizzly may have given him some ideas about a plan of attack:

> "As Putin rears his head and comes into the airspace of the United States of America, where do they go? It's Alaska. It is from Alaska that we send

those out to keep an eye on this very powerful nation, Russia, because they are right there, they are right next to our state…"

Yes, that's Gov. Palin back in 2008, showing off her foreign policy expertise and putting the responsibility for "sending those out" on Alaskans. WTF?! Putin's an ex-KGB assassin. If he comes for you, you'll last as long as a fifth of Stoli at a Siberian funeral. And look at how the Russian government translated Sarah's statement, according to Wikileaks: "Putin's rear, his head, where do they go in the airspace of my God I cannot understand a thing this woman is saying. Let's attack."

She can't think, but she can shoot. Real Americans know which of these skills is most important and when we go into the voting booth, we pull the trigger accordingly.

OR NOT

The 2010 mid-term elections were a watershed, a referendum, a refudiation, and other fancy words that mean it was a huge, unprecedented deal for the party of an incumbent president to lose congressional seats.[1] The Tea Party's effect on the outcome can't be overestimated, but we can try.

First, let's ignore the Tea Party candidates who lost. The rising tide of the far right didn't lift all boats. In fact,

---

1 *Happens nearly every mid-term, Boyle. Would it kill ya to research? If so, try it. (—ed.)*

some of the biggest boats sank like tea in a harbor, despite an energized voter base, NRA backing, and the best support money can buy, in the form of Palindorsements® and "Beck's Got Your Back"™ promotions on Fox News. So, as you lose your Second Amendment rights, remember to forget about these people.

Christine O'Donnell

Everybody loves Christine O'Donnell—both left and right appreciate her charmingly tiny intellect and big mouth—but

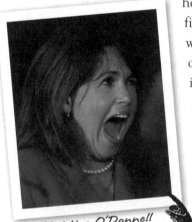

Christine O'Donnell demonstrates her non-masturbatory O-face.

her 2010 defeat just doesn't fit the narrative that began with her surprise victory over incumbent Mike Castle in the Republican primary. She was likeable, she had Tea Party bigwigs in her corner (and, as she put it, "Sean Hannity in my pocket"), she set Delaware fund-raising records, and she had a top rating from the NRA for her enthusiastic support of gun rights, including her innovative plan calling for a dildos-for-handguns swap to get America's youth "off the buzz" of masturbation. Plus, she had supernatural witchy powers, proven when she magically transformed campaign funds into rent money and bowling shoes. And yet she lost. Let's not think about this.

Carl Paladino

Carladino! A mob-boss look-alike and the loudest critic of gun control who ever ran for office in New York (location, location, location, Carl!), Paladino wanted to re-legalize assault weapons and teach school kids how to shoot them.

He also suggested a "final solution to the problem of fag marriage" that involved replacing rice/birdseed with bullets/hand grenades at gay weddings (this book may not have gotten the details there quite right[2]). He even once threatened to kill a reporter. The Tea Party, with its hatred of the media and love of threats, adored him for that, and for his charming way of saying, "If ya don't vote fuh me, I can't guarantee you'll be safe from the homos." And yet the guy only won 34 percent of the vote amid a GOP landslide. How could this happen? Let's not find out.

Would you buy a contract killing from this man?

---

2 *Why start now? (—ed.)*

Joe Miller

Hey, Joe, where ya goin' with that gun in your hand? Everywhere! The original Papa Grizzly, Joe Miller, drew crowds of armed supporters during his failed 2010 bid for the U.S. Senate, and explained his fellow Alaskans'

tendency to "come heavy" to rallies and campaign events as an expression of love for the Constitution. Miller did Carl Paladino one better by not merely threatening a journalist, but by actually slapping handcuffs on the guy. The Tea Party has rarely been so disappointed as when Miller dropped his legal challenge to the election result and became one of the few GOP candidates for

Joe Miller grows a beard in front of a live audience.

national office to be beaten by a write-in campaign. Alaskans later breathed a sigh of relief, as his campaign aides disclosed that if he'd won, he would have followed Sarah Palin's lead and quit the job early, citing a desire to spend more time with his stubble.

Sharron Angle

Nobody running for office in 2010 put the Second Amendment first the way Sharron Angle did in her heroic attempt to knock off Senate Majority Leader Harry Reid. In a radio interview, after implying that she was carrying a concealed .44 magnum, Angle spoke of "Second Amendment remedies," not only for the general problem of tyrannical government, but for the more specific "Harry Reid problem." It's the closest any national candidate has come to encouraging the assassination of a public official, except

Sharron Angle bathes supporters in the warmth of her rage.

for Obama's 2008 campaign against all white people, who, after all, hold most public offices. Angle also described denying abortions to rape victims as turning "a lemon situation into lemonade." How could she possibly lose? We don't want to know.

Tom Tancredo

The lone Palindorsed® loser to run on a third-party ticket in 2010, Tom Tancredo infuriated the GOP establishment by splitting the conservative vote and handing the Colorado governorship to a Democrat. Gross! In his defense, Tancredo is nuts (and in Colorado's defense he can still get a gun permit). A drum-beater for the Vietnam war in the '60s, he got a mental health deferment and went on to start an all-out war against other non-white people in his obsessive quest to shut down illegal immigration. Tancredo is a classic jingo-depressive narcissist whose American Constitution Party candidacy was admittedly "a goofy idea I had after going off my meds." (Disclaimer: this book did not verify that quote, and may have invented the diagnosis. This book does not research. It simply tells it like it is.) Tancredo would have watered the tree of liberty with all kinds of blood, so his loss is tyranny's gain. The damage to our republic is incalculable. Don't even try to calculate it. Don't think about it. Just clean your rifle and be ready.

Tancredo, one wacky whitey.

ELECTING STRAIGHT SHOOTERS

This book can't dwell on missed opportunities and losers. Real Americans always look on the bright side, even when we're squinting through a scope. A good way to see the mid-term election glass as half-full is to half-fill it with frosty, refreshing Rand Paul. Just look at him. He's like a thinner, gun-rights-supporting version of Alec Baldwin, full of opinions, self-importance, and medical training like Baldwin's character had in the film *Malice*, written by coke-addled liberal Aaron Sorkin. But Baldwin merely played a surgeon with a God complex. Rand Paul is a real eye doctor with omniscient vision.

Rand Paul

This book could run down a list of far-right victories in 2010 that would make liberal readers of this book cry like Hillary Clinton at a greasy-spoon photo op. But why bother when we've got Rand Paul, the toughest Republican since Tom DeLay, or maybe Michele Bachmann. But you won't find Rand Paul flailing around like a lavender ladyboy on *Dancing with the Stars* or showing off a new boob-job by standing at an oblique angle for TV interviews. Rand Paul (not just "Rand" or "Paul"—it's Rand Paul, and don't you forget it) is

all man, a Real American tearing Progressives a new one. He sets his sights on regulation and spending and evil, blasting away at them with every weapon at his command. With Dagwood-lookin' daddy-o Ron Paul covering the House, Rand Paul is moving into the forward area of the Senate, transforming that "deliberative body" into the right arm of God—and

A thousand-yard stare from an ophthalmologist.

apparently, the right arm of God is holding a gun, execution-style, to the head of big government.

Rand Paul opposes all forms of gun control. Period. This is a guy who sees no ambiguity in the Second Amendment. There's no wiggle room. There's no debate. Rand Paul is a straight shooter. With his ophthalmologically trained vision, he simply looks beyond the militia-related stuff in the first part of the amendment and applies pinpoint focus to the "right of the People" and the simple fact that the right "shall not be infringed." From this foundation he built the political platform on which he now stands like a sniper, firing away at the federal bureaucracy.

Rand the Man's Can-Do Plan

According to Wikileaks, or so this book heard, Rand Paul's first draft of a "100-Point Plan to Take Back America at Gun Point" includes these bold provisions:

➡ Send armed troops to destroy the Dept. of Education, the IRS, and the U.N.
➡ "Aiming At Schools" program: Every student shall be issued a handgun.
➡ OK, maybe they have to buy the guns. Note to self: consult gun lobbyists.
➡ Hey, what if gun manufacturers set up kiosks in schools?! Also, government can't tell business what to do, so gun sales may be denied on the basis of race.
➡ Oh, great, now the liberal media will call me a racist.

- ⇒ Have Rachel Maddow killed.
- ⇒ Strike that last one. It sounds sort of pre-meditationish.
- ⇒ The point is, students must be armed to protect themselves against teacher unions, trenchcoat Mafia thugs, and creeping socialism.
- ⇒ Is that 100 Points yet? I'm running out of ideas.
- ⇒ Note
- ⇒ to
- ⇒ self:
- ⇒ maybe
- ⇒ it's
- ⇒ a
- ⇒ 10-point
- ⇒ plan?

This is why Real Americans consider Rand Paul a more important figure in the Senate than his Kentucky cohort, Minority Leader Mitch McConnell. McConnell is a classic Washington Beltway insider. He'd never think far enough outside the box to fill out a 100-point plan by making every word its own point. Rand Paul is a poet-warrior! He's also handsome and expressive, whereas McConnell's face is made of wood and his voice sounds like an autistic robot. And remember how Rand Paul refused to shake hands after a campaign debate, saying, "I don't want to catch my opponent's liar germs"? That's the uncompromising spirit of dickness we need to take our country back.

KEEPING REAL AMERICANS' EYES ON THE TARGET

During the 2010 mid-terms, Sarah Palin's political action committee posted a map of the United States with gun-sight crosshairs over the congressional districts of twenty Democrats targeted by the GOP. She put it up on her Facebook page, too, and tweeted to her supporters to "RELOAD." At the time, a few wussy liberals complained about the crosshairs imagery, saying that it promoted violence against the targeted candidates. But all those candidates survived the election and liberals should shut up.

For example, Gabrielle Giffords (D-AZ) was among the congressional candidates targeted, but she won her race in Arizona's 8th District despite the Palindorsement® of her opponent, Jesse Kelly. Kelly's a jarhead nutjob who hosted a "Get On Target" campaign event where supporters could fire an automatic M-16 rifle as a symbolic gesture to "remove Gabrielle Giffords." Still, Giffords was re-elected, so where's the harm?

Oh. This book just remembered that three days after the new, 112th Congress was sworn in, while meeting constituents at a "Congress On Your Corner" event in Tucson, Giffords was shot in the head with a Glock semiautomatic. Six were left dead and twenty wounded by some kid who apparently had a beef about government mind-control. So there's the harm—if the government was controlling his mind, then this whole thing is Obama's fault. But another casualty of the mainstream media uproar over this tragedy is the largely-ignored fact that Giffords survived. She wasn't killed. Why? Because, as ever-vigilant Rand Paul explained a few hours later, "Weapons don't kill people." This book is not even making that up.

Sarah Palin, faced with criticism for posting the crosshairs map, released a video the following week accusing liberals and pundits of "blood libel" in their linking the Tucson shooting to her map and fightin' words. She first floated an aide's statement that her map's targets weren't crosshairs but "surveyors' symbols." When that was hooted down, she backtracked brilliantly, pointing out that candidates on both sides of the aisle used maps with targets on them.

How did liberals and pundits respond to her brilliance? Sure enough, they got their flowered undies in a twist over her use of the anti-Semitic term "blood libel." Some even had the audacity to bring up the fact that only *her* map put the crosshairs on Gabrielle Giffords. And of course, they were all over the shooter's mental health history like a straitjacket, asking pesky questions about how an obvious lunatic was able to buy a handgun and thirty-round magazines, or why, within days of the Giffords shooting, Glock sales skyrocketed in Arizona. Um, because this is America? Hello?

This is what we're up against people. Clearly, we'll never get the left to understand the importance of watering the tree of liberty with the blood of tyrants (or in this case, the blood of a moderate Democrat, a nine-year-old girl, and some other innocent bystanders). They don't get it. They'll never stop gunning for our guns, so it's important to keep the real target in our sights: selectively upholding the Constitution, keeping and bearing arms, and supporting Tea Party candidates who will do the same. That's what the People are doing out there in the Real America. Let's get out there with them and see how.

CHAPTER THREE

SEEING RED: A STATE-BY-STATE GUIDE TO TEA PARTIES (PART 1)

THIS IS THE FIRST of three geographical tours scattered throughout *The Tea Party Guide*. These chapters remind you that the Tea Party isn't just a movement: it's also a good time. Tea Party celebrations take place all across America, and these chapters will help get you there. So they're the most important chapters in the book. In fact, they're the most important chapters in any book, ever, except for that early chapter in *The Godfather*, page 26 or so, when Sonny and Lucy…wait… no. These are more important than that.

These chapters answer your question: *Where is the Real America?* by saying: *The Real America is everywhere.* Then you ask another question: *So how do we find the Tea Parties?* Then these chapters answer: *By reading this book! Man, you ask a lot of questions!* Then another question: *How do we know the people there are Real Americans?* Then Lucy's trembling hand closed on a blood-gorged pole of muscle…wait…no. We know Real Americans by their spoons. Their thimbles. Their shot glasses. Not their regular old everyday spoons, thimbles, and shot glasses, of course. We're talking collectibles.

Real Americans visit as many states as possible and bring back state-specific trinkets to relive the memories. That decorative thimble from Arizona holds a Grand Canyon's worth of fond memories. A spoonful of Vermont is all a Real American needs to hold the sticky-sweet syrup of dreams born there. And a shot of Minnesota will keep a patriot warm through the longest winter.

We're in luck as we traverse the jigsaw puzzle pieces that make our American quilt the melting pot that it is (metaphors are often mixed in the Real America). For in each of these thimble-/spoon-/shot-glass-denoted destinations, there's a party—and every American is invited to attend, to participate, to bellow through bullhorns, and to carry guns. All fifty states now participate annually in an honest-to-very-narrowly-defined-god Tea Party party! Some states (especially red ones, like those in this first installment) have more than one party goin' on. And not just small business owners and community-college dropouts in short-sleeved dress shirts waving signs and hoping to get on the local news. These are festivals, feasts, and week-long benders. These babies are full-blown blowouts like Rio's Carnival, without the skimpy outfits and headdresses (except for Massachusetts, as you'll see in Chapter 6).

Here's what Real Americans are up to. Red states, here we come.

ALABAMA

State Motto: "Almost Mississippi"
State Bird: The Yellowhammer
State Hammer: The ball-peen
State Song: "Sweet Home, Chicago"

All About Alabama

Alabama takes its position as First State In The Alphabet seriously, despite the fact that many residents don't understand the concept of alphabetical order. State license plates, manufactured throughout Alabama's thousands of prison facilities, proudly proclaim, "In Your Face, Alaska."

With its redneck ways, white-sand beaches, and blue-tick hounds, Alabama remains as patriotic as Lynyrd Skynyrd and as welcoming to outsiders as a Ku Klux Klan board meeting. Small wonder that this conservative, easily-riled state is home to not one, but *two* of the most exclusive Tea Party events in the country.

Sweet Home, Sweet Home Days

Every summer solstice in Birmingham, joyful participants sing and drink until the lines are blurred between those two surprisingly violent activities, and then the ceremonial Presentin' of the Papers proves that you were, in fact, born in the state. And so was your cousin. Don't even *think* there won't be some Skynyrd at this shindig.

Pray-Lean & Pee-Can Feast

Originally the Praline & Pecan Feast, but visitors to the Deep South don't know how to pronounce anything right. Huntsville's city fathers decided that the city mothers' delicious foods should not be sullied by mispronunciations of their ingredients, and have misspelled the name of this celebration so stupid Northerners won't say it wrong. The misspelling alone has attracted huge numbers of Teabaggers, who also like to pray, lean on stuff, and pee in cans. And they like to eat. Come early, because if you show up after sundown, it looks like a swarm of chubby locusts came through.

ALASKA

Nickname: Land of the meth-head son
State Flag: A mama grizzly recumbent on an oil spill
State Beverage: Vodka 'n' slush
State Tree: The log

All About Alaska

Alaska is Palin country. Oh, sure, Sarah Palin quit her job as governor before her first term was up, and she turned out to be kind of a ditz and a liar, but she's so dang pretty and her Family Values are so va-voom that everybody's just gaga for her.

Alaska is also Lady Gaga country. Not really. Not much of an impression made up here, to tell you the truth. But on

Ice Road Truckers one time, a Lady Gaga song came on this one trucker's radio, and he yanked the radio out of his dashboard and ate it, spitting out the harder-to-chew parts into his tobacco cup. So there's that.

But the main thing about Alaska is, it's a hotbed of the Real America. Guns and guts and axes and beards and beer. And look what happens up north every spring:

Inuit Accusation Festival

Having given up on proving that oil roughnecks, loggers, truckers, crazy homesteaders, and other stragglers were in fact the original residents of the state, Alaskans perform a program of essays, poems, songs, plays, and furious debate each spring that artistically demonstrate how much better off everyone would be without the so-called "native" Inuit hanging around. The festival culminates in the famed "Chase 'Em Onto An Ice Floe" run, in which all participants (except the Inuit, who seem fewer every year) are issued a sidearm. Big fun for the little ones, if they can avoid hypothermia.

ARIZONA

State Slogan: "Adios, amigos!"
State Food: Mexican
State Bean: Mexican jumping
State Antipathy: Mostly toward Mexicans

All About Arizona

Look, Mexicans, we know what you're thinking. You're thinking, boy, for a state with so many Mexican migrant workers and Mexican-Americans and Mexican cultural thingies, Arizona sure doesn't like Mexicans! You couldn't be further from the truth.

Well, you could be a little further. Why don't you try it? Go think that thought in Mexico instead of here in the US of A, because the truth is here. Then you'll be far, far south of it and Real Americans can get the jobs back that they really don't want. Everybody loses! Speaking of which, here's a coupla Tea Parties you don't want to miss:

It's Pronounced "FEE" Fest

Yes, it began in Santa *Fe*, New Mexico, but quickly spread across the border to Arizona, the way Mexico-associated stuff tends to do. This festival consists of an arduous, month-long focus on not pronouncing anything with even a hint of a Latin accent. Don't miss the "Take Out Tay-cos" which are like tacos, but half-priced if you say the name like a Real American should.

Losin' It with the Minutemen

Originally called "Hangin' with the Minutemen," this event lets regular citizens spend a day with the gun-totin' border militia whose patriots are named for their lack of sexual stamina. But Minutemen are notoriously unstable, and this one guy totally ended up hanging himself from the border fence, so that "Hangin'" name seemed kinda inappropriate after that. Today's festival brings bold young virgins from all over the state, seeking to "lose it" to a guy who won't make the initial discomfort last too long.[1]

IDAHO

State Song: "Flight of the Bumbling FBI Fugitive"
State Dangerous Sex Game: Scrotumdy-Peg
State Coen Brothers Quote: "Nice marmot."
State Flower: The automatic rifle

All About Idaho

To grasp America's precarious situation, take the drive from Boise to the town of McCall, high in the mountains of Chile, I mean, Idaho. The winding road makes you sick to your stomach, as sheer cliffs of terrorism fall away from dizzying heights above the river of national decline. A socialist is driving and there's no guardrail, and you're in the back seat of the big boat of a foreign car that is America. Who can blame you for peeing your pants? It's this kind of fear that makes every day a Tea Party in Idaho. Check it out:

---

1 *Did we say "from all over the state"? We meant, "This one crazy chick tried it." That's about it.*

Every Day's a Tea Party in Idaho Days

This year-long event is not so much a festival as a lifestyle. Parties are redundant in Idaho. If you've been there, you know. If not, you gotta go.

KANSAS

State Motto: *Ad Astra, Per Aspera* ("To the Stars, through Painkillers")

State Dilemma: Megachurch or SuperAngryMegachurch?

State Band: Alabama (used to be Kansas, but they were too progressive)

All About Kansas

It's flat, people. Sure, you got your Flint Hills to the southeast, but they suggest just how little the land has to do to be called a "hill" in this state. You've got your Rocky Mountain foothills on the western border, but they don't count because Kansas stole them from Colorado. It's this flatness that gave Kansans like Bob Dole and Dwight Eisenhower their identity. Bob Dole didn't put Bob Dole up on a pedestal or a promontory, because Bob Dole didn't have things like that in Kansas. Neither did Dwight, or "Ike," as he was nicknamed by his wife, Sweet Bob Dole from Pike. Kansas politicians used to be moderates, like those guys. Them days is over.

God Hates Fags Year

This loud, continual protest was started by vicious faux-Christian minister Fred Phelps, whose homosexual tendencies so disturbed him that he decided to take it out on the rest of the country, even heterosexual soldiers killed in wars he supported. Don't ask—but tell. Not about yourself, but about everyone else. That's the Kansas way.

Bird Month

The birthplace of basketball piggybacks on Indiana's annual gala (pronounce with short "a" sounds, princess) to celebrate the total whiteness of a true American roundball hero. Larry Bird was pale, slow, homely, and one of the greatest ever to play the game. This is how we win, Teabaggers. We stay within ourselves, give 110 percent, and come through in the clutch. For our country. For our children. Now get out there and party.

MISSISSIPPI

State Slogan: "Above all, consistency. Below all in everything."

State Fake Beard: Spanish moss

State Time-Counting: One-North-Dakota, Two-North-Dakota, etc.

All About Mississippi

When de Soto discovered Mississippi, he turned to his men and uttered these famous words: "Uh…let's go back." Thus,

Mississippi remained isolated for centuries. But a small enclave of famous writers, musicians, and performers (Faulkner, Elvis, Kermit the Frog) built the state's rich culture of writing, music, and dating pigs. Then carpetbaggers came in and wrecked the place. Now it's up to Teabaggers to pull up that carpet, reclaim this steaming, foreign-moss-draped land, and make of it an earthly paradise, where all are free to go to the worst schools in the country, and do stuff like this:

Good Ol' Fashioned Book Burnin' Time

Libraries burn as pickup trucks circle them, full of hooting, hollering locals and visitors who know that facts go away if you can't see them. Torches: $5. Funnel cake: $3.

SOUTH CAROLINA

State Tree: The dwarf palmetto
State Insect: The smaller-than-Florida's palmetto bug
State Nagging Question: Why is everything about us relatively unimpressive?

All About South Carolina

Crippled by mediocrity, South Carolina has never achieved its potential, which wasn't much to begin with. Dwarfed by its sister to the north and stepbrothers to the south and west, the lesser Carolina was already struggling when its cousin to the east, the Atlantic Ocean, sent a distant uncle, Hurricane

Hugo, for a visit in 1989. The state had barely recovered when a thirty-foot replica of the Confederate flag was discovered in the governor's pants, causing a scandal that cost the state millions in tourist revenue when everybody nice decided to stay away. A couple of reasons to reverse that trend:

Anti-Clam-Tax Clambake

This festive weekend not only marks the ongoing struggle to avoid the Clam Tax, but all other taxes as well. The catchy slogan, "Tell Washington to Clam Up!" is now forty-seven years old, but so pointed and accurate that it hasn't been beaten despite efforts from major Spartanburg ad agencies, three junior colleges, and a prison.

Not So Fast, Bitches! Parade

This slow procession through the streets of Charleston celebrates the half-century it took for South Carolina to ratify the Nineteenth Amendment and give women the right to vote. That's right, folks: they kept women's hands off the levers of democracy until 1973. Woo-hoo!

TENNESSEE

State Elvis: Presley
State Figure-Skating Elvis: Stojko, but nobody much likes male figure skaters here
State Naughty Bit: Pelvis

All About Tennessee

Look, Davy Crockett was from this great state—what more do we need for a Tea Party? Put him, Elvis, Aretha, and Dolly Parton together, and that is one sick Tennessean four-way, with a raccoon tail sticking out from somewhere we don't even want to think about. (*Ed. Note: Actually, we kind of do.*) Tennessee's claim to conservative fame was the Scopes trial, in which fancy lawyer Clarence Darrow defended a teacher who insisted on teaching evolution, breaking state law AND God's heart all in one semester. To make up for this sordid past, Tennessee Teabaggers should show up for stuff like this:

Hill-William Days

A statewide effort to be taken more seriously by referring to everyone named Billy as "William." Results have been mixed, but since anyone's failure to call a Billy "William" requires each of the parties to do a shot, everybody wins!

TEXAS

State Motto: "Austin ain't Texas, but it's here anyway."
State Song: Panhandle's "Messiah"
State '80s Fads Still Kickin': Line dancin', mechanical bull ridin', wife-beatin'

All About Texas

Ha! There's no way to tell you all about the great state of Texas in one puny li'l book! It's way too big! From its dusty plains to its Lyndon Baines to its piney woods to its smuggled goods to its Rio Grande to its somethin' land, Texas is a sprawling, bar-brawling, cattle-calling kingmaker of a state. Yep, they make kings here and export 'em to other countries, cuz Texans bow to no man! Except maybe to Bush family attaché James Baker or whoever rules the place when they finally ditch the rest of us puny Americans once and for all:

Seriously, We're Seceding This Time Festival

A good-natured effort to leave the Union marks the month of October in the Lone Star State. Join the former Texans as they make license plates into ashtrays and bow to the Governor/ King who sports a powdered wig and false beauty mole.

UTAH

State Song: "White Christmas"
State Minority: The rare and exotic non-Mormon
State Alternative Lifestyle: Monogamy

All About Utah

When Brigham Young brought his passel of persecuted polygamists over the Rockies and through the woods to the Great Basin of northern Utah, he could scarcely have imagined the church, city, and Mitt Romney of today. The gleaming spires of the Tabernacle look out over the streets of a Salt Lake City as clean and white as a fresh-scrubbed Mormon, which everyone on those streets pretty much is. It's without question the weirdest city in America, and positively teeming with Teabaggers. What do they do for entertainment in these parts? If by "these parts," you mean anything but genitals—which are forbidden by state law—here's an example of a Tea Party, Utah-style:

Rustic Springs Sing-Along Campfires

These impromptu events crop up "every now and again" just outside Rustic Springs and the melodic, ominous chants about the bright future will stick with you and recur at the weirdest times! Like when you can't sleep or are about to go under at the oral surgeon's. Hymn books: $5. Funnel cake: $3.

WYOMING

State Angst: Visitors might remember that Dick Cheney came from here

State Song: "There Ain't No Veeps from Wyomin'"

State Motto: "Dick Who?"

All About Wyoming

The Oregon Trail cuts a lonely swath through the vast prairies and craggy peaks of Wyoming, leading straight to the "Devil's Tower," where westward wagons met up with a gigantic-ass UFO and were never seen again. So settlers didn't really settle the area. That's why the ninth-biggest state in America is fiftieth in population. Like, nobody is out here. It's ours if we want it, and Teabaggers should want it. We need to remind this once-great state that its infamous, secretive, heartless native son Dick Cheney didn't ruin the country—liberals did. We need to pick Wyoming up by the scruff of its neck and shake it like a seizure, which is a popular dance at these fine Tea Parties:

Frack You! Fest

This party's a gas—literally. Teabaggers put up a makeshift hydraulic-fracturing rig, forcing water and toxic chemicals into bedrock to liberate trapped natural gas, benzene, and other carcinogens, allowing them to roam freely in Wyoming's formerly pristine waters. This is all legal thanks to the 2005 energy bill crafted by Cheney and his cronies. Don't miss the science demo where kids can light tapwater on fire. Cheneyhead drilling helmets: $5. Funnel cake: $3. Drinking water (bottled): $10.

Rowdy Railroad Revelry Days

The rails brought on brutal land disputes, the environmental devastation, the birth of forced immigrant labor, and the final defeat of the Indians' horse culture, so it's only natural to celebrate them here in Casper, the friendly ghost-town! Singing, dancing, local artisans, and visiting performers are all things they don't have in Wyoming, but the spike-biting contest makes this destination your destiny! Also, Dick Cheney is from here. 'Nuff said.

(Ed. Note: Is your red state missing from this sampling? See our online supplement at Teabastard.com for more Tea Parties, more fun, more Real America!)

CHAPTER FOUR

WE'LL BE THE JUDGES OF THAT

THIS BOOK HAS ASSERTED that everything used to be good, but now it's not, because everything-ruiners (i.e., liberals, progressives, socialists, secularists, and stinkybuttists) have made it bad. America is still great, of course, but its greatness is in jeopardy, which is a challenge, because you always have to answer in the form of a question.

So there you have it—that's what's wrong with Progressivism. It doesn't have answers; it only has questions. But why? Why are liberals always asking and probing and questioning assumptions and ruining? What is it that Real Americans fear about the Progressive Agenda? What is the Tea Party all about, for $50, Alex?

The Tea Party is all about judgment. Freedom is important, and so are lower taxes and gun rights and everything else that's in this book, but before you can even talk about those things, you have to know what you're against. You must judge, which means to divide right from wrong, like Solomon slicing a baby in half. That should be easy, but liberals make it hard, because they don't like the idea of right vs. wrong. They're always mixing things up, hedging, weighing this and that, slicing the baby in at least three pieces. They're always stirring the pot, instead of shitting or getting off it (pardon this book's French).

That's it—liberals are like the French. In the French judicial system, they don't just make a distinction between crimes and misdemeanors—that would be too black and white. They have a third, in-between category where it's a little worse than a misdemeanor, but not as bad as most crimes—you know, not a nice thing to do, but not so horrible, eh, who can say— let's break for coffee and cigarettes and sex with someone else's spouse. That's France, home to all kinds of bad, Progressive ideas.

Montesquieu, a French judge notorious for fuzzy verdicts and oral technique.

The Progressive agenda in this country is about breaking down our sense of right and wrong, trying to render our judgments moot. That way, they can do as much wrong as they like and make it seem right. But what are these wrongs? How do we know they're wrong? How can we stick to what's right, when we're beset on all sides by wrongness that's made to look right by the mainstream liberal media?

YOUR ONE-STOP COUNTRY FOR VALUE SHOPPING!

That's where Real American Values come in: **God**. (Love that Guy!) **Country**. (USA! USA!) **Business**. (Especially minding other people's.) **Money**. (Can't get enough of it!) **Family**. (We're for it—but only if it's built around the marriage of one man and one woman who has no control over her reproductive destiny.) And, of course, **Guns and Television**. (Time for a break yet? This book wants to watch *The Deer Hunter* on cable.) These values made this country the greatest on Earth. And, as noted in Chapter 1, the absence of those values is why other countries suck.

The Soviet Union could have been the greatest. They had it all: huge oil reserves, superb potato-distilling technology, and a frightened, obedient population. Where did they go wrong? No values. Being godless commies, their God, Country, and Family values dissolved in corruption, crime, and Hot Russian Brides with live chat and photos of beautiful Russian singles and Ukraine Girls in lingerie at hotrussian-brides.com join free for dating! Its Business values are shot, too: Russia's state-run oil industry is the laughingstock of fossil fuel profiteering, and its spills, though numerous, aren't as impressive as those we enjoy in the United States. Money? Government spending bankrupted the country. Finally, to amplify the theme of Chapter 2, despite strict commie gun control, Russia's murder rate is four times higher than America's. Many of those murders take place as Russians are doing shots of the national drink while watching the depressing national news, so they clearly misapplied the Guns and

Television value. This proves that guns don't kill people, bad television does.

To sum it up: Russia is wrong and bad. But it's easy to judge. The important thing is to apply good, American values to every issue. You'll be right every time. Better yet, godless liberals and dirty socialists will be wrong.

THE WRONG AND THE SHORT OF IT

What are liberals and socialists so wrong about? Everything. But we can't have a chapter about everything, because then it would be bigger than this book itself, causing the universe to implode. The following formula shows how to apply values to a few key issues:

[ISSUE]	⇨	Dirty Socialist Position	⇨	[VALUE]	⇨	Tea Party Position

This gives us a quick Move to the Right, through a value that divides wrongness (theirs) from rightness (ours). Here's how it works on a short list of issues:

TAXES	⇨	"Give us your wealth so we can support you in your poverty."	⇨	MONEY	⇨	Taxxed Enoufgh Allredy!
GAY MARRIAGE	⇨	"Preach love, not hate/Sodomy is really great."	⇨	GOD/ FAMILY	⇨	"It's Adam and Eve, not Adam and Steve! Or Steven."

TERROR	⇨	"Why do they hate us?"	⇨	COUNTRY	⇨	"Clinton caused 9/11!"
HEALTH CARE	⇨	"Big Brother knows best, as advised by Anthony Weiner (D-NY)."	⇨	BUSINESS	⇨	"Get your government out of my Medicare. And your Weiner out of my Twitter feed."
GUN CONTROL	⇨	"Sarah Palin's Facebook page kills innocent people."	⇨	GUNS AND TELEVISION	⇨	*"Sarah Palin's Alaska* is awesome!"

That's how values get Teabaggers to the right side of an issue. Now, you may find it hard to see how a value like Country can lead from the Dirty Socialist Position of questioning terrorists' hatred of Americans to the Tea Party Position that Clinton caused 9/11. Allow this book to explain: Country is, of course, a value based on the love of America, but it's also a call to personal responsibility, which Real Americans accept if it's convenient. Assigning Clinton the personal responsibility for 9/11 is a way of expressing love for this country. Make sense? No? Well, then consult one of Ann Coulter's books. They don't make sense either, but they'll confirm what this book just told you.

Not that anything here needs confirmation! You know we're headed for a Democrapocalypse. You don't have to back it up. Being a Real American means you don't depend on "facts" or "research" or "reason." That stuff gets in the way of judgment. Judge first; figure it out later, if ever.

That's what Real Americans did about New York's "obesity

taxes" in January of 2009, staging the first modern-day Tea Party protest at the local level, although the people attending the event were so fat, it spilled over into surrounding states.

That's how CNBC journalist Rick Santelli sowed the seeds for national Tea Party fervor on February 19, 2009, with his famous trading-floor rant about the federal government "promoting bad behavior" by "subsidizing losers' mortgages." See how Santelli judged both the government and home-buyers in one sentence, with no thought about the role of profiteering banks? And because he was ranting—not thinking—he could just toss out a half-assed solution that would accomplish absolutely nothing: a so-called tea party for traders to dump mortgage derivatives into the Chicago River. With thought replaced by judgment and anger, we other non-thinkers could cheer him on and start putting together the first nationally-coordinated Tea Party events.

Thought-free judgment gave Keli Carender, a young

Angry feebs and bitter crones await the Democrapocalypse in our nation's capital.

Seattle conservative (a rare, exotic species) her idea to protest the 2009 stimulus bill, calling it a "Porkulus Protest" after the Rush Limbaugh–coined term combining "stimulus" and "pork." She continues to put a fresh face on the Tea Party, with her nose-piercing, hipster eyeglasses, and upbeat attitude, contrasting sharply with the angry feebs and bitter crones who form the core of the movement. There are lots more like her. Well, several. Okay, maybe a couple.

WHO'S FERTILIZING THE GRASSROOTS OF THE ASTROTURF?

If you're not always sure what to be against, then listen to those who are. Remember, though, the Tea Party isn't some monolithic brainwashing machine that renders all your judgments for you. It's lots of individual brainwashing machines, unified only by a shared spin cycle on Fox News and a laundromat to steam and press Dick Armey's lobbying money. As we saw in Chapter 3, there are scads of Tea Parties across the broad face of this great land. So, you may ask, is there astroturf war among the grassroots? If so, who do I side with? Who's really in charge? Well, the short answer is: nobody. The long answer is: the following nobodies.

Nationwide Tea Party Coalition
These patriots fueled the first Tea Party protests in 2009. Newt Gingrich later joined the steering committee, which has a goal to "make only right turns until we get wherever Newt wants us to go, because our collective IQ barely adds up to his, I mean, Jesus, he knows everything." Other groups coordinate their efforts via this coalition, and they all follow

Newt on Twitter. The guy tweets like a magpie, exhorting his minions and spouting opinions like this one from December 2010: "Senate gop has more than enough procedural tools to stop harry reids lame duck power grab and force adjournment through echaustion" (sic). Who said that a high IQ had to be an impediment to good old-fashioned Tea Party misspelling?

Tea Party Nation

This group sponsored the National Tea Party Convention in 2010, offering grassroots ticket prices of $549 and paying Sarah Palin $100,000 just to show up and wink into a microphone. Tea Party Nation was founded by Tennessee lawyer Judson Phillips, who advocates rolling back voting rights to the original Constitutional provision: only property owners get to vote. Doesn't he sound like a great guy?

Tea Party Express

This is the famed national bus tour dreamed up by a Republican consulting firm, organized by their political action committee, and fueled by sweet diesel, baby. In a beautiful, self-sustaining ecosystem of cash, the PAC behind the Tea Party Express has funneled more than a million bucks to the consulting firm that gave birth to it, while dropping the occasional nickel on political campaigns. Former TPE chairman Mark Williams nearly derailed the whole thing (yes, it's a bus that runs on rails—they're still working out the kinks) with his racist blog, but was quickly given the boot (an expensive parting gift, usually a mukluk stuffed with cash). And TPE co-founder Howard

Kaloogian is the former congressional candidate whose campaign website posted the famous "quiet street" photo as proof that America had brought order to Iraq (the street was actually in Turkey). So these guys know what they're doing.

The National Tea Party Federation

Not much is known about this shadowy, johnny-come-lately group that formed in 2010, but the word "Federation" is a tip-off that it's probably a front for liberals masquerading as Real Americans. They further gave themselves away by expelling the Tea Party Express from Federation membership over the Mark Williams racism fiasco. That is just soooo PC.

Tea Party Caucus

This is the brainchild of Michele Bachmann, who's been heard to ask, "What's a caucus, like a prayer meeting?"[1] Forty-eight other Republican representatives have joined her alleged caucus, responding to her promise "to bring cookies and wear that push-up bra you guys like." Several Tea Party activists accuse Bachmann of hijacking the grassroots movement from The People, but as she explains, in her native Bachmannese, "The Tea Party is a big tent, except not like one of those FEMA tents which are an abomination unto the Lord and that's why I don't fill out U.S. Census forms, and you shouldn't either unless you want to live in a FEMA concentration camp under Obama's socialist martial law." Ooookay then.

---

1 *Ironically, Bachmann has tested negative for a brain. (—ed.)*

Liberty Central

This is the group founded by Ginni Thomas, the wife of Supreme Court Justice Clarence Thomas. She's the woman who threw her weight around (which is dangerous—carnival guessers estimate her at 350 lbs.) and demanded an apology from Anita Hill for all that "Long John Silver, pube on a Coke can" stuff during the Senate confirmation hearings for Big Clarence's nomination to the Court. Anita declined, but Ginni Thomas's outrage has bigger fish to fry. She's now stepped down from Liberty Central leadership to do full-time lobbying, so it remains to be seen if this group's influence will wax or wane. As a big Bush supporter from 2000 on, Ginni herself hasn't waxed in years.

Tea Party Patriots

The "Official Home of the Tea Party Movement" claims more than one thousand affiliate groups across the country. It was founded by Jenny Beth Martin and Mark Meckler, who galvanized crowds at the 9/12 march on Washington, if "galvanized" means "left 'em wanting more clichés from better speakers." Their heroic efforts in 2010 were rewarded with a million-dollar gift from "an anonymous donor" (Dick Armey's FreedomWorks). They promptly hired a professional staff, including Seattle nose-piercer Keli Carender, and a Washington, D.C., public relations firm. This is also the group that pushed the "Contract From America" (see ten "planks" below), demanding that federal lawmakers sign it as a pledge. As of this writing, the only signatories are Senators

Tom Coburn and Jim DeMint, who are illiterate and can't be held responsible for anything they sign. Take a look at the Contract, in ten slightly revised planks:

1. Identify constitutionality of every new law, and make sure that the ones we don't like are judged unconstitutional.
2. Reject emissions trading. In fact, reject global warming. For that matter, reject the globe.
3. Demand a balanced federal budget, unless it means cutting defense spending, because yikes Muslims yiiiiiiikes.
4. Simplify the tax system. Vague enough for ya?
5. Audit federal government agencies for constitutionality. May have to create a federal government agency to do this. Audit that agency. Uh-oh. Infinite bureaucracy loop.
6. Limit annual growth in spending. Also, can you check this growth on my neck?
7. Repeal health care legislation passed on March 23, 2010, even though the non-partisan Congressional Budget Office projects $150 billion in savings. We only believe CBO projections when they fit our ideology, dude.
8. Pass an "All-Of-The-Above" Energy Policy, or whatever.
9. Reduce earmarks. Also, skidmarks.
10. Reduce taxes. Duh.

Note the emphasis on constitutionality. This book will devote furious attention to the U.S. Constitution later on. For now, hark unto the blunt, fabricated words of Supreme Court Justice Antonin Scalia: "If it ain't in the Constitution, it ain't shit." And then that Liberal Bastard John Paul Stevens uses his stupid ol' logic on Scalia's remark to prove that if it *is* in the Constitution, it *is* shit. And then Scalia's, like, "Find me the shit in the Constitution, you old fart, point to it." And Stevens is all, "Okay, how about the part where Negroes are legally considered three-fifths of a person, you textual-ist twit?" And Scalia gets really pissed and pulls a Beretta, and Stevens tries to run away and falls on his ninety-year-old ass, and Scalia stands over him and says, "I'm gonna tell all your civil-rights-lovin' liberal friends that you said 'Negroes.'" And Stevens cries.

While we're judging, we must judge the Contract From America incomplete. It's a few bricks shy of a load, in terms of getting everything judged. To do that, we need to trowel on a few more issues:

11. Entitlements (bad)
12. Pork (bad, except for projects in your own state) (and bacon)
13. Immigration reform (bad, unless it's done the Tea Party way)
14. Activist judges (bad! unless they're conservative)
15. The Media (lamestream liars, except for Fox)
16. Science (mostly wrong) and secularism (totally wrong)
17. The 112th Congress (House: so far, so good! Senate: still bad!)
18. Iran (evil!)
19. North Korea (crazy-evil!)
20. Obama's birth certificate (forged!)

TO BE JUDGMENTAL, OR NOT TO BE JUDGMENTAL—THIS IS A QUESTION?

You may have noticed that the issue of abortion is not on the list. That's because it's controversial, even on the right. Some Tea Party leaders (i.e., Sarah Palin) have proclaimed it wrong under any circumstance, including rape, incest, or life-and-death situations for women. This has some Teabaggers asking: really? Isn't that a little nuts? Arguments ensue. Fights break out. Guns get pulled. You'd think such a basic issue would unite the right in a powerful throng of pro-life, anti-abortion judgment. You'd think *Roe v. Wade* would be black and white. But in fact, it's Blackmun and White.

Harry Blackmun is the Supreme Court Justice who wrote the 1973 *Roe v. Wade* opinion, finding "a right to privacy" in the due process clause of the Fourteenth Amendment and bossing states around, telling them what kinds of laws they can't pass. Byron White wrote the dissenting opinion. He and William Rehnquist were the only two Supremes who stuck to the obvious intent of the founding fathers: to tell the founding mothers what to do. Jeez, women couldn't even vote back when the Fourteenth Amendment

Justice Harry Blackmun (bad!).

was written, much less make decisions about their reproductive organs.

You may ask: "Mommy, what is the Due Process Clause and why does it kill babies?" If your mommy is a Real American, she'll say something like this: "Well, dear, the Fourteenth Amendment says that no state can 'deprive any person of life, liberty, or property, without due process of law.' Subsequent cases established that the government can't place an 'undue burden' on the 'right to privacy' and the 'right to make decisions about highly personal matters' BECAUSE ACTIVIST JUDGES HATE BABIES!

Justice Byron White (good!).

The words 'right to privacy' don't exist in the Constitution! How can you have an undue burden when you have a due date?! Obama is the baby-killer in chief! Quick, hide! Black helicopters!"

So. The only thing we all agree on is that nobody agrees on the Fourteenth Amendment with regard to abortion. All we know for sure is, it was a Blackmun day for America when seven out of nine Supreme Court Justices turned out to be liberal activists.

This book does not recommend arguing about abortion within the Tea Party ranks, because sooner or later, a pro-lifer will kill somebody over it. Best to reserve your judgment for some of the other issues listed in the Contract earlier. Here are a few quotes from Tea Party stalwarts to beef up your talking points and sound like a Real American.

On the Media:

"I suppose I could play their immature, unprofessional, waste-of-time game, too, by claiming these reporters and politicos are homophobe, child molesting, tax evading, anti-dentite, puppy-kicking, chain smoking porn producers…really, they are…I've seen it myself…but I'll only give you the information off-the-record, on deep, deep background; attribute these 'facts' to an 'anonymous source' and I'll give you more."

—Sarah Palin

NOTE: You might want to stay away from "anti-dentite." Whoever writes Sarah's emails used this old *Seinfeld* reference that describes someone who is a bigot toward dentists. It just makes you sound kinda batshit.

On the Science of Climate Change:

"You got to have an enemy to fight. And when you have an enemy to fight, then you can unite the entire world behind you, and you seize power. That was Hitler's plan. His enemy: the Jew. Al Gore's enemy, the U.N.'s enemy: global warming. Then you get the scientists—eugenics. You get the scientists—global warming. Then you have to discredit the scientists who say, 'That's not right.' And you must silence all dissenting voices. That's what Hitler did."

—Glenn Beck

NOTE: If you can compare a politician, institution, or anybody you hate, to Hitler? Do it. It never gets old. Notice how Glenn throws 'eugenics' in there, so it sounds like he knows about science. Eugenics has even less to do with global warming than it does with stem-cell research, which is his usual target when he brings up eugenics. Just throw in random concepts like "string theory," or make up crap, like "job-killing eco-industrial green energy complex" and you'll sound like an expert, when really all you're doing is using scare tactics, JUST LIKE HITLER.

On North Korea:

> "They're a major threat. I just think it would be fun to nuke them and have it be a warning to the rest of the world."
>
> —Ann Coulter

NOTE: Keep it simple. The "it would be fun to nuke them" approach is underused, because most people care too much about their credibility to use it. Ann shed her credibility long ago, freeing her to simplify any issue and throatily snarl whatever comes into her alleged mind. That, friends, is *How to Talk to a Liberal (If You Must)*.

On Obama's Birth Certificate:

> "We're getting ready for the communist takeover of America with a non-citizen at the helm."
>
> —Michael Savage

NOTE: Because he supports some environmental causes, advocates good nutrition, and has a Ph.D., radio host Michael Savage is no Tea Party darling. Plus, his real name is Weiner, which sounds Jewishly suspicious and junk-tweeting. But he's a wackjob at heart, and sometimes embraces a right-wing issue to the point of humping its leg. He was all over Obama's citizenship like a TSA frisk, and you should be, too. Nothing infuriates liberals more than delegitimizing their celebrity leader.

IN SUMMATION

When a court judge brings down the gavel on a verdict, the defendant is either guilty or not guilty. There's no sort-of-guilty, but wait, sort-of-not. Extenuating circumstances may affect the sentencing, but the verdict is what it is. Up or down, good or bad, *Deal or No Deal* with your host Howie Mandel. Either the prosecution has prevailed, or a bleeding-heart ACLU lawyer has once again freed a criminal to roam our streets.

The Tea Party is not afraid to judge. We're afraid of the things we're judging. And we're way more passionate about what we're afraid of than what we actually want. Our fear quickly turns to rage, and as we sort out what we're so pissed off about, out comes the judgment. Bang, the gavel of our far-righteous indignation comes down.

Then we're off to a rally. Now that you know what you're protesting and why, it's time to talk about how. The following chapter will help Tea Party newbies fit in with protest veterans. It'll remind us all to stand up for what we believe against. That's the Real American way.

CHAPTER FIVE

OH, YEAH? WELL, METHINKS I DOTH *NOT* PROTEST TOO MUCH!

A HEAPIN' HELPIN' OF handy tips on how to protest (and how not to), with an appetizer of rollickin' verse, a side of racial politics, and some tasty rally pictures for dessert.

THE BIRTH OF A TEABAGGER. A POEM.

O, big was the bosom of brave Roland Boyle,
And bigger his Chevy, which burned lots of oil,
And biggest his heart, which was angry and swollen
With patriot's pride like a pizza-clogged colon.

It was pizza for breakfast—cold pizza and porn
And cleaning his guns on a cold April morn—
That inspired our hero to stop, lock, and load,
Pack the heat in the truck, put the truck on the road,
And drive to a protest on Tax Day, 'oh-nine,

The day true conservatives all grew a spine—
The day all the bailouts and bounced checks came
   due,
And the Tea Party threw something new in the brew.

He'd just paid his taxes, and Boyle was steamed.
His rate had come down, but he'd still gotten
   creamed.
And the Senate had just passed that stimulus package,

A big, stinking heap of Obama's Barackage.[1]

He was driving from west Independence, Missouri
Through east Kansas City. He had reason to worry.
On this side of town, nice trucks were a rarity.
No place revealed economic disparity
Quite like the east side—the land of the hoopty,
Where nobody bothered to scoopty the poopty—

---

1 Not sure this is a word, but you get the idea. The photo shows our alleged
president and OMB Director Peter Orszag planning the financial demise of the
country. The big fruit bowl seems to be saying, "How do you like them apples?"
And the Tea Party (not pictured here) seems to be saying, "We don't."

The ghetto, the projects, the welfare-state mess.
How anyone lived here was anyone's guess.

What happened, Americans? Where the hell are ya?
You need shaking up. What's it take now to jar ya
Awake? All our pensions and 401(k)s
Are as gutted and gone as those long-ago days
Growing up in the 'burbs in our innocent youth,
The U.S. fat and strong, like cigars or Babe Ruth.
Or Theodore Roosevelt, tough and rotund.
We were never outflanked or outfoxed or outgunned.

We didn't start wars. If we did, we would win.
And no way would some guy with the middle name
    "bin"
Ever pull off a stunt like September 11.
If he had, we'd have hunted him 24/7.
That dude would be dead with his head on a pike,
If we only had leaders like Teddy or Ike.[2]
Boyle'd voted for Bush (twice!), which now seemed
    insane,
And then he'd defaulted to lamebrain McCain,
Whose campaign fell flat—might as well have been
    shelved
When it turned out his running mate's IQ was 12.

2 *The 2011 assassination of bin Laden apparently means that Obama's more "like Teddy or Ike" than Bush was. (You're welcome, Boyle. —ed.) For what? Burial at sea? I wanted bin Laden's head on a pike, not in a pike! (—RB) (Pike is a freshwater fish, Boyle. Try to grow a brain before your book tour, OK? —ed.)*

Looking back, Boyle felt stupid. Eight years of
    Bush/Cheney
Will do that, he thought—and he'd never been brainy,
But even a dropout like Boyle understood
What those guys left behind was a pile of no good.
Mission Accomplished? Still mired in Iraq.
Still in Afghanistan, but not in the black.
Still bailing, still spending. Still a hole at Ground
    Zero.
If the U.S. was Rome, Bush/Cheney'd played Nero.

The truck hit a pothole and bounced, as Glenn Beck
Blared forth from the radio, angry as heck.
Boyle's thoughts swerved to health care reform.
    Jeepers Christ.
If Congress went commie, they all should be iced.

His buddy, Brad Wankoff, had vowed to revolt
If a mandate was passed. Boyle patted his Colt.
Brad was hard-core right wing and a firearms
    enthusiast
(His Glock was the Glockest, his Uzi the Uziest).

It was Wankoff's idea to come "stand up for freedom."
He'd said, "Fight the socialists, bro! We can beat 'em!
Show up at the Plaza. Bring guns. You may need 'em.
We'll scope out some betties. Who knows, we might
    meet 'em!"

(That prospect, not protest, kept Brad off the couch.
He hadn't been laid since the Reagan years. Ouch.)

To mid-town went Boyle. It got quieter, quite—
Less bumpy, more fancy, and way, way more white.
Boyle drove past the Nelson (the famed art museum—

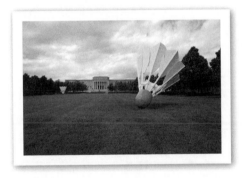

You could see fartsy arts there, but who wants to
see 'em?)[3]

Those dumb pop-art shuttlecocks—shuttlecock *this*,
All you hoity elites in your toity abyss…
Was the Nelson tax-funded? Boyle figured, hell yes.
The building could pass for the damn IRS.

---

3 *Actually a world-class art museum, and privately-funded. (PS: There are*
nudes in there, Boyle. —ed.) It figures. Filthy NEA-supporting liberals! Guess
I'd better pay a visit and check in on the declining morality of this once-proud
city. (—RB) (Good idea. Maybe there's even a docent's tour for Philistines and
rubes. —ed.) Shut up! (—RB) (No, you shut up. —ed.)

He flipped it the bird as he parked. A dark cloud
Was billowing grimly and threatening a crowd
Now gathering there at the end of the block.
This must be the rally. It looked like a flock
Of poncho-clad blimps with American flags
And signs about freedom and, yes, "God Hates Fags,"
And Obama as Hitler, and "Don't Tread On Me,"
And someone was warbling, "O, say can you see…"

This here was America. This rally was *it*.
Proud patriots fighting for freedom 'n shit—
Just to yell showed commitment. To turn out today,
In this weather, for media scorn and no pay?
That showed heart. It showed moxie, chutzpah
    and balls.[4]
Now Boyle waded into the crowd. In the scrawls
And the stencils and smeared magic marker of signs,
The shouts and the murmurs, the laughs and the
    whines,
Every guy on a donuts-and-rhetoric bender,
Boyle saw hope like Obama could never engender.
It was thrilling to think that a movement had
    started…
Just then, by the fountain, some patriot farted.

---

4 *Brand placement! This book is represented by the law firm of Moxie, Chutzpah
& Balls.*

It was Wankoff, an M-16 slung from his shoulder.
He looked crazy, or gassy, or maybe just older,
Holding a protest sign hurriedly scribbled
With "Nancy Pilosy can blow me!"—more ribald
Than Brad ordinarily was, but the spelling
Was very Wankoffian—and it was telling
That Brad had the Speaker so high on his list
Of Democrat bastards at whom he was pissed.
Brad was easily swayed by the latest on FOX,
Where Pelosi was bullet points: • bitch and • Botox
And • tax-and-spend liberal! Or • socialist harpy!
• Worst House Speaker Ever! And • Crazy! And
    • TARPy!
Since 2006, Brad had ragged on her ass—
But Boyle kinda wanted to tap it, alas.
Elaborate fantasies…Nancy…aw, jeez…
In a lather, in leather…so lithe…what a tease…
Face down…on her back…in the truck…on her
    knees…
Now Nancy astride…now a Nancy trapeze…

"Hey, Boyle!" It was Brad. It was back to reality.
Whew. Roland Boyle's secret shame was a malady
None in this crowd, he was sure, entertained.
He could never tell Brad how Pelosi had stained
His libido. His wife, his best friends, no one knew
That Boyle's passion for Nancy burned red-hot—
    or blue.

He turned away slightly, adjusting his crotch.

Something splashed in the fountain. The men
  turned to watch.

There were people, all whooping and hollering now,

As a couple of guys in white wigs took a bow

On the edge of the fountain, then dumped crates
  marked "TEA"

In the water. Boyle laughed, and then looked up
  to see

Some cops on the rooftops of shops down the way,

Their binoculars trained on the teabag melee.

They had rifles with scopes. ATF? FBI?

Boyle couldn't see who, but he thought he knew why.

And here came the Plaza security guards,

Pushing through like a crew of fun-spoiling ree-tards.

More tea made a splash. There was jostling and
  swearing.

Boyle looked up again, still getting his bearings.

He thought, oh, this crowd could get ugly
  (redundantly),

Second Amendment rights leveraged abundantly…

This was one big militia…but marksmen on roofs?

A bullhorn was bellowing, "We hold these truths…"

And Boyle, wet and cold in the drizzle and mud,

Had a vision of horsies and fishies and blood—

The big Frenchy fountain they stood by, awash

In some splattery hell from Hieronymus Bosch.
Pelosian images vanished. Instead,
A dead pool of patriot gore filled his head,
As a voice (maybe Hannity's) solemnly said,

"A Tax Day Tea Party. The waters ran red!"

And, shaking off visions of violence and Eros,
Boyle said, "It's no time for us to be heroes."
He dragged Brad away as the crowd milled and
    seethed
'Round the fountain some millionaire magnate
    bequeathed
To a town that had once claimed "More Fountains
    Than Rome"
And that Boyle now escaped. He and Wankoff
    drove home.

Ah, home. Boyle's house was a ramshackle shed
Where he found himself sitting, half out of his head
With post-rally emotions and pre-mixed mojitos,
A grill full of burgers, a mouthful of Cheetos—
Reflecting on, really, what rallying meant.
It suggested a comeback. Making a dent,
A diff in the way that the USA went.

Boyle squinted at Wankoff, passed out on his lawn:
Where's Middle America, man? It's real gone.
Just look at the bill with which Washington's
    stuck us.
The middle had better start raising a ruckus—
Or the lower and upper are just gonna fuck us.

And sitting there, hammered, with smoke in his eyes,
Boyle thought: it ain't pretty, but politics-wise,
If you look past the loony-tunes, racists, and lies,
This Tea Party thingy might just be the shiz-nit—[5]
And that's what America needs right now…iz'n it?

LET'S REVIEW

The preceding is a drunkenly embellished account of a
Teabagger's first exposure to "the movement." One name has
been changed to protect a guy this book knew back in high

---

5 *Pretty sure that's the way we talked back in '09. (Fo' shizzle, Boyle-dawg!
—ed.) Fo' shut up, Snoop-editor! (—RB) (No, you fo' shut up. —ed.)*

school, the kind of guy you'd see at a rally with a misspelled sign and a Glock 9mm under his poncho, if not an M-16 strapped over it. Sometimes the truth must be bent to the exigencies of verse, to enliven the proceedings and promote the general gaiety.

The point of all this is that protest does take real commitment. You gotta want it. Bad weather, bad company, and bad restrictions on our First and Second Amendment freedoms all conspire against you having a good time making vague threats to government officials and firing your gun into the air the way you like.

And there are some weird tensions that few Teabaggers really care to address. We want to come heavy to rallies, but would prefer not to get our heads blown off. We want to express our anger, exercise our rights, and hold our government accountable. Nobody pays attention to protests, though, unless there's a sufficient number of us doing it. But we're individualists, and we don't really trust groups unless everybody in the group looks and thinks pretty much like we do—which paradoxically undercuts our individualism. And we don't like paradox. We prefer hypocrisy. We champion the Constitution, but don't really want to think about (speaking of general gaiety) the equal protections it guarantees to gay people. Right-wingers have to be dragged kicking and screaming into pooping the Party by suggesting that gay marriage is actually a constitutional imperative, unless that right-winger is gay libertarian Andrew Sullivan, who probably likes kicking and screaming, but who's about as likely to show up at one of our rallies as he is to sponsor a NASCAR team.

The Tea Party has to figure out how to put up a big tent. The problem is, the bigger the tent, the more idiot campers it can hold.

TOLERANCE, US?

We're stuck, then, with zombie homophobes like Westboro Baptist preacher and cryptkeeper, Fred Phelps, whiny racists like ex-Tea Party Express director Mark Williams, and a lot of other people who make our flesh crawl.

Even though we're suspicious of words like "tolerance," which we know to be a cause of moral decline, we have to tolerate the far fringes of our movement. What else are you gonna do, shoot 'em? If you took out all the crazies, you'd run out of ammo pretty fast. This book hates to admit it, but we might learn a little something about inclusiveness from our counterparts on the left, who pride themselves on diversity. There's strength in numbers, even if it means a higher number of dopes who make us all look bad.

That's worth remembering as we look at How To Protest. As individualists, we each have our own way of expressing outrage, including our own way of spelling it. This should be celebrated, not shamefully ignored or denied.

You don't have to be able to spell "government" to protest it. But after the first Tax Day protests, when photos like this were splashed all over the Internet, the liberal media used them to promote the idea that Teabaggers are idiots. The suggestion is that if it weren't for bad education, the Tea Party wouldn't exist. Oh, yeah? Well, where do you think we got that bad education? In public schools, run by the "GOVERMENT"! We have to defend our idiots, people. They're fighting the very thing that made them stupid.

We've all seen the famous photo of Teaparty.org founder Dale Robertson and his "racial epithet" sign, right? You'd be seeing it here if this book could get publishing rights to it. When that didn't happen, the question arose of how to communicate the crudeness of this photo and others like it. And the answer came: hire the great cartoonist, Revilo, to do a visual "re-enactment" of the moment! It's like re-enacting the Civil War, only with ink instead of nerds! Nobody renders idiots quite like Revilo. Here's his sensitive portrayal of Dale Robertson and that less-than-sensitive protest sign pressed closely against his star-spangled blubber.

The liberal media made a meal of the original photo, feeding it to every lamestream outlet in an obvious attempt to discredit the entire movement. But this tubby Teabagger doesn't represent conservatives' racial sensitivity any more than Sting represents liberals' abilities at tantric sex (Exhibit A: Harry Reid).

While the image of the Senate Majority Leader doing the yab-yum is stuck in your head, let's rethink that allegedly offensive sign. All Dale Robertson did was equate the relationship of Congress and taxpayer to that of slave owner and slave. The racial epithet refers NOT to African-Americans, but to us all, in our servitude to a rapacious Congress. Plus, it's misspelled, so it's not even the same word! Spelled this way, it would rhyme with "cigar" and sound like a chocolatey French dessert. That's not offensive! It's classy!

Does that argument hold up? Frankly, this book can't tell, because it can't get the horrifying image of Harry Reid out of its mind. The truth is, the Dale Robertson imbroglio is hardly an isolated incident. Let's face it, Teabaggers, we have some bona fide racists in our midst. You may recall another rally photo of a pasty Teablubber boy with his racial terror on display, rendered here as the cartoon he obviously strives to be:

Sorry, but that's just hysterical white-boy paranoia, which is never as effective on a protest sign as it is coming out of Glenn Beck's mouth.

We have to face the country music on Tea Party racism, folks. Don't deny it. You've seen the signs protesting health care reform with Obama in medicine-man regalia. You've seen Obama as a Black Panther, as a swarthy jihadist, and as Urkel, the nerdish black sitcom character, with a scrawled magic marker caption saying something like, *"What you talkin' 'bout, Willis! Spend mah money?"* Uh-huh. Look, if you're going to carry a sign about Obama's blackness, here's a tip: *Be black.* Granted, if you're black, you're probably not Tea Partyin'. The few black 'baggers among us like it that the president is black, but dislike his policies. Take a cue from them, white people. If you think freedom of speech means spewing stupid racist ideas, it's time for…

A QUICK, TWO-STEP COURSE IN RACIAL POLITICS

Step 1: Acknowledge that you were born with a huge white leg up, here in America, where white fortunes were built by slaves and immigrant labor, putting non-whites behind the eight-ball for centuries as whites ran the table and used every form of oppression, violence, and Jim Crow crapassery available to do it. Sure, race relations have improved, but we're only seven generations out from slavery. It's been barely a dozen years since white supremacists dragged James

Byrd to his death behind a pickup truck just for being black in Texas.

Even today, despite achievements that include a Kenyan Muslim winning the presidency, non-whites still struggle against all kinds of institutional and personal racism. Stop blaming black and brown people for your problems. Being born white is the second-best predictor of economic success in America, right behind being born rich and still ahead of being born Oprah or LeBron James. We have a long way to go until the freedoms promised by our Constitution are fully, equally shared by Americans of every color. Until then, if you really want to advance the cause of conservatism in this country, please advance to Step 2.

Step 2: Shut the hell up about race.

But wait, the reader may say. Didn't this book rag on Obama for kissing white women, back in Chapter 1? Yes, it did. Isn't that racist, asks the reader? Yes it is. This is a humor book, so it can claim to be ironic, using cheap jokes to send up the racism evident in right-wing politics. That's way different than an angry skinhead holding up a sign that says, "Stand Up for Equal Whites"—or worse. Also, this book can't help noticing that the reader just ignored Step 2 by continuing to talk about race. Please refer back to that important step and shut the hell up.

WOW, THIS BOOK GOT ITS UNDIES IN A TWIST THERE FOR A SECOND

Consider that li'l digression an extra "Don't" from *The Tea Party Guide*'s Do & Don't list of Protest Etiquette, which goes a little something like this:

DO:	DON'T:
Carry guns. Exercising your Second Amendment rights shows government who's boss: the NRA.	Fire them into crowds or into a congress-woman, even if Sarah Palin gave you the idea.
Carry the flag. It's a symbol of the hard-won freedom we stand for.	Carry the Confederate flag. It's a symbol of slavery. We're for freedom, stupid, not slavery.
Carry a copy of the Constitution.	Read it aloud. It's actually kind of boring.
Dress up like the colonists of 1773. This connects us to the original Boston Tea Party.	Be rockin' too much cleavage, Dolly Madison. The repressed sexual energy of right-wingers can't accommodate your bodacious rack.
Carry a cell phone and/or camera. Document the activism!	Document the racism. Like it or not, showing these diverse points of view may not help our cause.
Carry a cooler full of snacks and energy drinks. Stay peppy and chubby.	Complain about having too much to carry. Jesus carried the cross for you, right up to the top of Capitol Hill. Man up.
Carry a protest sign.	Carry a really stupid protest sign, like this next one...

Again, this is a rendering of an actual Tea Party rally photo. Revilo has lovingly captured the guy's faux colonial costume and his sheepish look as people apparently tell him to put his really stupid protest sign away and maybe go back to school. The original photo must have been shot in low light through a lens smeared with grease from freedom fries or something. It simply wouldn't reproduce. Let's hope the guy holding that sign doesn't, either.

WHICH KIND OF WRONG IS RIGHT?

See, it's one thing to spell "dissent" with one S or two I's. We could call that creative spelling and defend this numb-skull's right to protest however he sees fit. But to spell it "descent" is just too low a denominator; it obscures the meaning. Then he compounds the error by getting the quote wrong—dissent isn't "the highest form of patriotic." That's like saying, "Shittie grammer is the highest form of idiotic." Get a brain on, pal.

The other problem with this quote is that it comes from the left. People attribute it to Thomas Paine or Thomas Jefferson, but there's no evidence for that. The earliest attribution is the Friends Peace Committee, a bunch of commie Quakers who posed it as a question in 1961: "Is dissent the highest form of patriotism?" Howard Zinn, a filthy liberal historian, was the first known blowhard to use it as a declarative sentence. Now, maybe you don't care where it comes from; maybe claiming that Jefferson said it is good enough for you. If so, a tip of the three-cornered hat to you and your shameless misattribution. That's how we Real Americans free ourselves from the tyranny of "facts" and rewrite history to support our rage. If we didn't have the Founding Fathers giving us our talking points, all we'd have would be Fox News. Speaking of which, here's a famous Tea Party rally sign, from a photo that appeared all over the Internet, but rights to which could not be secured for publication, not that this book is bitter about it or anything:

THANK YOU FOX NEWS FOR KEEPING US INFROMED

Yes God Bless America

Yes, "INFROMED." Liberals have had a good laugh over this, assuming it to be a dyslexic version of "informed." It's not. This is a new, three-syllable word, sort of like "infrared," pronounced "in-fro-med." It carries the meaning of "informed," while describing a new technology developed by Fox News during the debate on Obamacare. "Infromed" technology gave conservatives up-to-the-minute "in"formation on Obama ("fro") and his socialist plan for a government takeover of health care ("med"). Infromed.

PROTEST AND THE HEALTH OF OUR REPUBLIC

Ooof. This book just pulled a groin muscle, explaining that sign. Good thing America has the best groin health care system in the world—and that's why it's so important to take back the Senate. The House is already moving to repeal

Obama's unconstitutional attack on our freedom to be the thirty-seventh-healthiest developed nation on earth, and our freedom to spend twice as much for health care as, say, France or Japan, both of which have universal coverage and are WAY healthier than we are, despite their respective diets of snails and eels. We outspend everybody on health care, because we're number one! USA! But with Obamacare, those costs could come down and Luxembourg could spend more than we do! They're only a thousand bucks per capita behind us now, with universal coverage, and they can afford to spend more because they have the world's highest average income. Luxembourglets (kids) are covered until they're twenty-seven! Luxembourgluglugs (drinkers) have the highest alcohol consumption in Europe! Their costs gotta go up! Do you want to be number two in health care spending behind dinky, drunken Luxembourg? We have to push these costs to the breaking point, as a matter of national pride.

A conservative Senate majority in 2012 could pass a repeal bill and let the free market in health care do what it does best: find innovative new ways to thin the herd. (We're currently twenty-fourth in the world in life expectancy, but that's in regular years. Remember, American years count for more—they're almost like dog years.)

As the political rally season blooms in the spring of 2012 and the rhetoric begins to warm the air like cancer-causing sunshine, let your voice be heard on health care and other important issues listed in previous chapters. Hoist your protest sign proudly.

If you were educated in our crummy "goverment"-run public schools, though, try to avoid words that you know might trip you up. "Socialism" and "Socialist," for example, have been famously botched by Tea Party nitwits protesting "Obama's Scholiast Health Plan" and others declaring that "Socalism Is Unamerican." Like it or not, people may think you don't know what socialism is if you don't know the word itself. They may not listen as you explain that our socialist public schools educated you poorly. If your protest is about the federal budget, remember it's not the debt "sealing," it's the debt "ceiling." That's "i before e, except after c..." Oh, forget it. Just find a magic marker with spell-check.

Here's a cautionary patriot for you. She at least got her health care protest right (there have been plenty of "Reapeal" and "Repeel" signs out there). But come on, lady. How are you going to protect our "Counstition" and our "Rebublic" from liberals when you're providing so much ammunition—or is it amuintion—to shoot you down? It's like you're auditioning for a role on a show about the ignorance of Teabaggers, written by Hollywood elitists, starring Neil Patrick Harris as a log cabin Republican, with you as his brain-injured mom, who tries to "pray away the gay" but gets ignored by God because her prayers are so badly worded.

SO. Maybe you don't need to know how to spell stuff in order to protest it or protect it. But there comes a point of diminishing returns on stupid. You can take your COUNSTITIONAL freedom to be an idiot too far. DESCENT like this is not the HIGHEST FORM OF PATRIOTIC. Despite wearing a shirt with a flag on it, you may undermine the REBUBLIC for which it stands if you can't even get the basic terms of your protest right. This is a Teabagger who needs an intervention. She needs this book to slap her upside the head and say, "You're doing it wrong."

When you do it wrong, you make a mockery of all Real Americans, especially in Fake American places that already look askance at us. We're going to some of those places now. So be ready to do it right, in the lion's den of the left.

CHAPTER SIX

Don't It Make My Blue States Red: A State-By-State Guide (Part 2)

DON'T BE FOOLED BY so-called blue states, patriots. Yes, blue goes with more things than red, if you're concerned with fashion, which, why are you? And yes, most jeans are blue and cowboys wear jeans and cowboys are possibly the last true Americans (except for the *Brokeback* ones). But blue has fallen on hard times of late, which should be no surprise to historians—blue has been the wrong color since the war between the states.

Manifest destiny, however, requires that we acknowledge these "states." And that's destiny, and it's manifest, so there's no way around it, which is the whole point of manifest destiny in the first place. It's the dream of the forefathers that America be just too big to ignore, so let's not start lopping parts of it off, as much we'd like to. We're looking at you, Hawaii.

Anyway, most of these prodigal arbitrary land masses actually have lower divorce rates, less domestic violence, and better test scores than their redder betters. So one thing is clear: they lie about being married, fighting, and ciphering. But if you look hard enough, you'll find right-thinking people, just like you do in prison and so-called mental institutions. And Congress. "Seek and ye shall find" is a comforting phrase that, together with this guide, may help you find the oasis of Tea Partydom in these places:

CALIFORNIA

State Bird: The Subpoena
State Salad: All of them
State Role Models: Various Kardashians

All About California

To many, California represents the American Dream writ large. These are people who don't know how to spell "written" and do not live inside the consequential United States Those of us who call this our terra firma know two words in Latin and also know that California is just what happens when you take a state from someone else and fail to totally wipe that someone out. Lesson learned.

The Tea Party is beleaguered here, especially near the urban centers. But there's a fun event in L.A.—the unlikeliest spot except maybe Berkeley or Alcatraz.

Hays Office Days

A week-long return to the "real" Hollywood, when innuendo and accusation and outright lying ruled the day and an ankle was too much skin! A highlight is "Black List Tuesday" when a random celebrant is labeled a communist, beaten, and fired, sometimes with actual fire, Santa Ana winds depending. Sexual abstention is encouraged but, after all, this is California. We can only do so much.

HAWAII

State Nut: The coco

State Ho: Don (Daniel Ho is actually cooler and has five Grammies, but hey, "Tiny Bubbles")

State Drum Solo: The original *Hawaii Five-O* theme and "Wipeout" (tie)

All About Hawaii

These people get both the most beautiful spot in the South Pacific AND states' rights in the US of A? Explain to this book how that's fair. And then they go and exercise their states' rights by enacting tough gun laws. They should be shot, but we know that won't happen, because they have the lowest incidence of gun violence in America—if you call that American.

Anyway, it's hard to get people up and protesting when their lives are so relaxed and pleasant, but if you can pry them off the beach, some Hawaiians get angry enough to qualify as Teabaggers. Then try dragging them to this luau:

Pigs, Pineapples 'n' Poi pLatter Days

Note the intentional miscapitalization on the word "pLatter," tipping you off that this is a pre-apocalyptic event, sponsored by Mormon missionaries. Festival-goers enjoy Glenn Beck videos and survivalist demos as a roast pig, pineapple skewers, and poi are served in the crater of an active volcano. The actual volcano site changes from year to year, so the police and parks service never know where we'll strike next on our suicidal quest to rapture out of here before things really go bad. It's kind of like a rave, but without the drugs. So, really, more like a prayer meeting with hula and trichinosis.

ILLINOIS

State Fish: The freshwater Capone

State Pizza: "Chicago" style, originally designed to feed up to seventy-five immigrants, now serves one Bears fan…barely. Laugh-beer-through-your-nose pun intended.

State Irritant: Singing P-E-O-R-I-A to the tune of G-L-O-R-I-A. Drives 'em nuts.

And Speaking of Peoria: It's used as a "middle America" testing ground for many products. Which explains the universal disappointment associated with so many products.

All About Illinois

Illinois is, of course, some kind of Indian word that means, "we're calling it this just to rub it in." Home to an impressive amount of creative politicking that makes it seem less like a state and more like a violent musical without songs, Illinois is actually comprised of two parts: Chicago, where bad things happen, and The Rest of Illinois, where they don't. Don't miss this big do in Springfield:

Lincoln Would Have Been a Viciously Conservative Republican If He Were Alive Today Days

You'd think this revisionist-history festival would be self-explanatory, but public officials here seem unable to get with the program and celebrate the GOP's claim to Lincoln's legacy. We have to teabag 'em into submission. With its central location, its neglect of the Emancipation Proclamation, and its thrilling Assassination Friday feature, this event could be the "Abe's Head" to the "bullet" of your Tea Party itinerary: not to be missed.

MASSACHUSETTS

State Adams: Sam. John was kind of a dick.
State Boat: That piece of crap your brother-in-law said he'd fix up and keep in his heated shed which turned out to not be heated or a shed but just some pallets stacked up near a power plant cyclone fence.

State Mystery Disappearance: The letter "R" among Bostonians (exception: at the end of the word "idea").

All About Massachusetts

This state should be Tea Party central, but aside from some reenactments and some actual tea (yecch), this is one of the most godforsaken bastions of liberalism on earth. With colleges on every street corner of every town, it's wall-to-wall eggheads here. It tells you a lot about a state when it's all but impossible to spell its name. Even Mississippi has a little song to help you out. Try to spell Mississippi without singing in your head. You can't! Now try to imagine a song set to the idiotic M-a-s-s-…achusetts. It just makes you mad, and that figures because righteous anger was invented in Mass-a-whatever, and is celebrated at the following…

Goody Good Fest

Fun for the whole family, as women who are hotter than the women who accuse them of witchcraft are, you know, accused of witchcraft. Then, the hot women get even hotter when they're humorously burned in effigy. Or in their trailers.

Goody Proctor: Doth this fest occur in Salem?

Goody Goodman: Yea, verily, but closeth on Sundays.

Sponsored by Sam Goody's. (Not really.)

MICHIGAN

State Slogan: "Our magnesium compounds will make you forget about our limestone quarries!"

State Union: Brotherhood of United Hey! Look Over There! (An influential employee empowerment lobby dedicated to ignoring things like practices and policies, stuff like that. You'd just be bored with it, really. We're doing you a favor.)

State Excuse: "*You* try working on an assembly line when you're as drunk as I am."

State Tribute Band: Seeeeeeger! (Still working on their night moves, but not bad.)

All About Michigan

There is a rebirth of patriotism in Michigan that is directly tied to the recent success in making American cars that Americans want. Since the bailout, GM has gone from losing $4,000 on every car made to earning more than $2,000 per car. This was accomplished by making the cars as much like Japanese cars as possible, while not-so-subtly suggesting the obvious conclusion that buying Japanese is un-American. Well played, Michigan!

Pantry Party!

Hours of fun as canned goods are labeled and stored in storm cellars that are impossibly thinly-veiled bomb shelters for when…well, never you mind. Just grab a label maker and join the Cold War-style fun! (*Ed. Note: Don't you miss the Cold War? We sure do. We miss home-canned peaches, too. This party has it all, except for a guarantee that you won't get botulism.*)

Beach Blanket Bailout Bingo Bonanza

This alliterative festival takes place on the shores of Lake Michigan—or maybe it's Lake Huron, but it sure as hell isn't Lake Superior, because that would be WAY too ironic for a Tea Party in protest of federal tax dollars bailing out the state industry. Festival-goers are each issued a beach blanket with a bingo grid on it. First contestant to fill it out and shout "Beach Blanket Bailout Bingo!" gets a tour of GM, including a PowerPoint on how taxpayers may actually make a profit on the sale of company stock. Earplugs provided so you don't have to hear about it.

MINNESOTA

State Lie: The 10,000 lakes thing is off by quite a few. You totally lose track trying to count them, like when you're little and try to count stars. So the claim is cute, but pointless (which was the state motto from 1897 to 1972).

State Prank: The Twin Cities often date the same suburb, sometimes getting as far as third base without her guessing.

State Nagging Feeling: That something in the lake is touching your leg, and it's not algae.

All About Minnesota

Fine. Prince is from Minnesota. But to be fair, lots of states have musicians from them; it can't be helped. Jewel is from Alaska. Alaska! Jewel! So you really can't hold Prince against us, although of course he'd like that. It was more than fifty years ago and we haven't done anything you can pin on us since. Plus, we've got this:

Only Child Left Behind Days

For three weeks in April, anyone who has only one child is singled out and ostracized because of the self-evident principle that normal people would want to have lots of children, and that white people, which Minnesota is full of, should! Because look at, like, Africa. They're having way more kids than we are. We've gotta have lots, Teabaggers! "Be fruitful and multiply" isn't just something God said so He could watch Adam and Eve do it. It's our Christian duty to propagate the herd. Get with it.

NEW YORK

State Dog: Boiled and sold to you on the street

State Solvent: Water used to boil state dogs

State Ploy to Take Your Mind Off the Smell of Urine: Calling one of your tallest buildings the nickname of your state. It's like a frat boy naming his penis. Sad.

State Mountain: Trash three weeks after pickup day

All About New York

Teabaggers like New York more since 9/11, but it's still a little too culture-y for most of us. Little-known fact: New York City was designed to be so utterly horrible, so completely unlivable, that would-be immigrants would turn tail and sail home at the sight of the imposing skyline and stern green woman threatening to set their boats on fire. What a failure. Since then, New York has continued to let America down something like seven times for every light on Broadway. Music, theater, "fine" arts, they're all there in New York. Inexcusable. But at least there's this:

Hooker Scrubbin' Week

Traditionally, the week before Fleet Week, and, surprisingly, the week after. Bring some rubber boots, a hose, and a long handled broom and get ready for a delousing good time!

OREGON

State Redundancy: A trip to Portland

State Shame: Grunge (wait, that's Washington...not easy to tell 'em apart, dude!)

State Shame (B): University of Oregon's mascot is a duck. No kidding. Ducks.

Every Other State's Shame, Related to Oregon: Sometimes being beaten by Ducks

All About Oregon

The most interesting thing about this state isn't whether it's pronounced "Or-e-gawn" or "Or-e-gun." That's third, after, "Why isn't it just more Washington?" and "Why is Washington a state and a city?" Oregon is distinguished by how much it hates people from California, but can't stop watching them in reality shows or unauthorized sex tapes. Portland is hellish, but to the east, you get Idaho's influence, which means stuff like this:

The Running of the Liberals

Scooter vs. Hummer is the recipe for this challenging event. Hummer wins. Hummer always wins. Ha, ha, ha, ha hahaha... (ellipsis to imply laughter goes on for a while, and gets that kind of evil genius sound, like a guy with crazy hair and a lab coat, you know the type?).

This Land Is Portland Music Festival

Why put a patriotic music festival in a liberal cesspool like Portland? Because it's "ironic." You can barely hear the Sousa over the catcalls, but every year, more feisty conservatives show up to sing along sincerely. And loudly. You could be one of them.

RHODE ISLAND

State Brain Teaser: Finding your home on a map.

State Excuse: "I didn't realize we had to wear pants on the island."

State Currency: Kidding! They use American money. But the fact that you almost believed it is telling, isn't it? Isn't it?!

All About Rhode Island

Is anybody fooled by the superfluous "e" or the silent "h"? Seriously? If you mean road just say road, you pretentious East Coast jerkoffs. You diminish us all with this charade. And if you read that, "char-odd," then no kidding, we're going to come over there and serve your chowder or whatever other goofy expression you've made up. Jerkoffs.

Shrew Tossing Days

Like its idiot cousin, Long, Rhode isn't really an island. But there are waterfalls to toss shrews over, if you like that sort of thing. Woonsocket Falls is a nice little town with a cool name, but then, they said the same of Sodom and Gomorrah. There are probably Rhodes scholars here, too, and that's bad. Still, if you want to hit Tea Parties in all fifty states, you might consider Shrew Tossing Days. Bring thick gloves.

WISCONSIN

State Slogan: "We Were Going to Go with the 10,000 Lakes Thing, Thanks for Nothing, You Lying Minnesotan Bastards"

Other State Slogan: "We Also Kind Of Look Like a Mitten, Thanks for Nothing Michigan"

All About Wisconsin

Brett Favre did not get the idea to text a picture of his li'l quarterback in Green Bay—they want you to know that right off the bat. For one thing, it's too cold, and for another, he's not even from Green Bay.

This state would be in play more often, or maybe even be a dependable red state, if not for the hyper-liberal town of Madison. Famous for cheese and cheese hats, Wisconsin also made a play to be famous for crackers until some of the wiseasses in stupid Madison started giggling about it.

Ice Hole Days

The fish are biting and the locals are perplexed at the annual rush to buy Ice Hole hoodies and Ice Hole beer cozies and

I'm With Ice Hole T-shirts. Bars stock up on the Flaming Ice Hole, which is a shot you do not want to miss.

OK, Teabaggers. Now that we've survived the sexy blue states, we can broach a delicate subject. Wrap yourself in latex, lube up, and hit that next chapter.

CHAPTER SEVEN

SEXUAL POLITICS:
TEABAGGIN' IN THE BEDROOM

SEX IS A NASTY gift from God. Because many conservatives were raised in repressed, religious homes, they may not receive this gift until they get married, if ever. But if they do unwrap it, they apparently enjoy using it. A recent study shows that people who consider themselves conservatives have more satisfying sex lives than their liberal counterparts—especially if the liberal counterparts are their wives.

But let's face it: the Tea Party is sexually conflicted. Many of us were taught that sex was a temptation of the devil, that being "good" meant denying these powerful urges, and that if we kept playing with it, it would fall off. These messages penetrated our unconscious minds, thrusting powerfully into our attitudes as adults, pinching the nipples of our prejudices, and spanking the ass of our fears. The anti-gay stance of many on the right makes us look prudish and tight-sphinctered, when we're really just selectively quoting scripture (Leviticus 18 or 20 something). Since many prominent anti-gay figures on the right (e.g., former Idaho senator Larry Craig, former RNC chairman Ken Mehlman, former minister Ted Haggard) have turned out to be gay, there's also a suspicion that anyone who speaks out about homosexuality is just wearing a fig leaf of bigotry to hide a throbbing dirty secret.

In 2002, GOP Attorney General John Ashcroft spent $8,000 in taxpayer money to have an aluminum "Spirit of Justice" statue draped, so its firm, uptilted right breast wouldn't steal the show at his press conferences, as seen here.

A pair of boobs in the Department of Justice.

This book searched high and low for a photo of the draped statue but couldn't find one, which is why you're forced to look at this filthy picture. The "Spirit of Justice" statue is nearly thirteen feet tall—that's bigger than Neytiri, the sexy Na'vi played by Zoe Saldana in James Cameron's blockbuster film, *Avatar*, a liberal, pro-environment, anti-American movie that no one should ever see—and look at the jug on Justice here! This Art Deco hooter is heftier than both of Neytiri's lean, athletic-looking bluebies put together. Adjusting for distance, that thing is the size of Ashcroft's head. No wonder he wanted it draped. What the media failed to note in its biased reportage of this story is that he also wanted to deliver his press conference remarks from behind the drape, and that his notes on the matter mentioned "a sweet mouthful of aluminum-num." The guy just wanted some time alone with Justice. Can you blame him? Well, yeah, you can.

LEAD US NOT INTO TEMPTATION... UH-OH, TOO LATE

We conservatives fear the power of sex, because we've seen how it can taint political careers and ruin lives. The very word "taint" is scary to us. We'd rather not think about it. We often perpetuate this psycho-sexual conflict by passing fears on to our own children. Why do we do this? Why saddle the pleasures of adult life with all this guilt and shame? If the word "saddle" just gave you a strange, quivering thrill, you probably have an especially pressing need to get these questions answered. Let's start at the beginning, with the people who messed everything up for the rest of us.

Not Adam and Steve.

Our human legacy of original sin gave us the knowledge

of our nakedness (Genitals 3:7), linking sex and shame forever. God punished our founding fuckers by expelling them from Paradise and cursing women with menstrual periods and pain in childbirth.

It was eating from the Tree of Knowledge that caused their downfall. Knowledge is bad! And Satan is the smartest, wiliest knower of them all. He tempted Eve; she tempted Adam; and the rest is Creationist history. This is why public funding for sex education is not only fiscally irresponsible, but morally corrupt. Kids don't need to know anything about sex, except not to do it!

Yet, from early childhood, we're naturally curious about the horrifying body parts involved and the strange sensations issuing from them. We want to know how it all works. We hear other kids talk about sex and are amazed that they don't explode or get hit by lightning. They say the word "screw" and we try to imagine how The Man can spin around as he drills into The Woman. We hear about fellatio and cunnilingus and 69 and we think, really? People do that? Can they even look at each other afterwards? The whole thing seems crazy and silly and embarrassing and please, tell us more.

HOW SEX WORKS

When two Real Americans love each other, they get married, which is a holy covenant sanctified by God and His Church. The church is like a bride married to Jesus (Second

Corinthians 11:2), although as far as this book knows he was a confirmed bachelor, which is why Martin Scorsese's *The Last Temptation of Christ* was so offensive to anyone who believes that Jesus was as chaste as his virgin mother, and don't even bring up that scholarly stuff about how the word "virgin" is a mistranslation from Hebrew, because if you're going to sit there and imply that Mary and Joseph got it on, you're going to be grounded for a week—wait, what? Oh. You wanted to know how sex works. Well, when two married Real Americans love each other very much, they hold each other close in a hug that only an adult man and an adult woman can do, and if you try to do it before you're married and old enough, it could kill you and you'll go to hell. From this special hug, you were born. Is that clear? Don't ever ask again.

That's the right explanation. But to hear biologists tell it, sex is just Nature using us for its own nasty purposes. We're all just collections of hormones and reproductive organs, trying to propagate the species. In fact, scientists say that if not for the primary male sex hormone testosterone, human life on this planet would never have existed.

That's a diagram of a testosterone molecule. Notice how it produces the word "OH" at the top. That's like "OH GOD

YES, TESTOSTERONE, DO ME NOW." The chemical formula for testosterone is $C^{19}H^{28}O^2$—a combination of Margaret Cho, the Steely Dan song "Hey, Nineteen," a 28-day menstrual cycle, and two balls.

WHAT IS THIS THING CALLED TESTOSTERONE?

It's balls, man. When people say "that guy has balls," it's usually not because he's juggling. It's because he's done something gutsy, something dangerous, something that you'd probably never do unless you had testosterone flowing through your endocrine system, bathing your brain in an androgenic bubble bath like a chemical lobotomy. Androgens are a more general group of steroidal compounds, of which testosterone is the most prominent—the one with the biggest balls, you might say.

Testosterone comes from the testicles, see, in the same way that patriotism comes from the heart. That's not to say that women don't have testosterone; their ovaries crank out a little, too. In fact, if a woman's libido drops off, and her husband complains when she says, "Not tonight," and he begs and pleads, and she says, "get away from me, one-track mind," and he says, "I think you should see a doctor," and she says, "I think you should shut up," but then she goes to see a doctor, the doctor may prescribe a testosterone-building medication of some kind. Testosterone makes you want to boink.

What else could explain it? No sane person would ever have sex if he or she didn't have a biological compulsion. It's messy, it's germy, and can cost anywhere from $50 for a quick pop to $1,000 an hour for a skilled courtesan, or so this book has heard. Our hypersexualized contemporary culture has some effect on our desires, of course, with its images of shaking booties and chiseled torsos and Salma Hayeks everywhere we look. Sometimes it's hard to know whether one's fiery urge to mate is hormonal, Hayekian, part of God's plan, or just Satan telling one to do bad things. Sex is a conundrum, a mystery, an enigma wrapped in a vagina.

The testosterone that fuels our need for it is also responsible for other forms of social aggression, so it actually helps Real Americans express their anger. But have you ever noticed how sometimes you'll be mid-protest, yelling about socialism or whatever, and suddenly you'll notice a really good-looking fellow Teabagger, and the energy goes out of your outrage? Maybe she's bending over to pick up a copy of the Constitution she dropped; or maybe his forearm muscles are rippling as he hoists a sign high overhead. You think, wow, I'd like to socialize *that*. Suddenly, you've forgotten everything else.

Biology crowds out political science. You find yourself grinding your teeth, making growly-grunty noises under your breath that sound like you're in pain. Lust is agony. Sex is a problem, and it gets in the way of solving other problems, such as entitlement spending or immigration reform, or even making fun of Nancy Pelosi who you suddenly realize was probably kind of hot when she was younger, and it disturbs you to think of her in that way, and you hate yourself, and now you'll never be able to look at her without imagining her at twenty-two, just out of college, vibrant and svelte and without the plastic surgery, smiling, energetic, Nancy running naked with you along the golden California shore, her skin bronze in the sun, her hair swinging, her firm young breasts bouncing to the rhythm of her long-legged stride and the surf and the sand and please excuse this book, it has to go to the bathroom.

POLITICS MAKES BEDFELLOWS

Because of testosterone, most of us spend a lot of time and energy thinking about sex, trying to have it, having it, or wishing it had been better after we've had it. As we know, it can be a disruptive force. For the Tea Party, which often seems a simmering cauldron of religiously-contained sexuality, it's important to learn to channel this energy into achieving what we might call a political *activasm*—an ecstatic release of zeal that can inseminate our movement with the potent jizz of anti-government fury.

Failing that, we should at least be able to hook up with Tea Party hotties.

To pull in the firm, nubile youth vote, we have to dispel conservatism's anti-sex vibe—and it looks like the Tea Party is doing just that. Did you know that the rallies of 2009 and 2010 resulted in dozens of marriages, thousands of dates, and untold numbers of sexual encounters, many of them producing Teababies? Interviews with Tea Party couples reveal that the political ferment of the last few years has been as effective as any dating service. If you don't believe it, check out these testostimonials from Real Americans across the country.

Tina N.
Loudonville, Ohio

"Paul and I met at a Tax Day rally in 2009. I was instantly attracted to him, partly because he was carrying an assault rifle, which gave me that 'I'm safe with him' feeling. But he's also really handsome. We made out in his truck afterwards, and when he didn't push my head down into his lap like most other Teabaggers I meet, I knew we'd be together. We got married six months later, and three months after that, along came a little tax deduction. Just think, this family wouldn't exist if not for Rick Santelli."

Tom Z.
Lee's Summit, Missouri

"As a youth minister, I admit to a weakness for younger women. At a town hall uprising in 2009, I was so angry I couldn't see straight, and mistook Gina for a twenty-something babe. She's actually seventy-six years old, but still hot as a pistol. I'm forty-eight, which, if you add the state of arousal times two, becomes the number of states in our great nation! People always call us 'George and Barbara.' I thought George Washington's wife was Martha, so I don't really know what they're talking about, but apparently we make a nice couple."

Molly W.
Robindale, Minnesota

"I met Steve at a fundraiser for Michele Bachmann. Instead of a speech, the idea was for Rep. Bachmann to do a *Girls Gone Wild* routine for a certain pledge amount. I think I distracted Steve, because we left before she even showed us her tits. All I remember from that night is him making a joke about inserting his amendment into my legislation, and me saying let's invoke cloture for a floor vote, and Steve looking confused."

Dan T.
Chicago, Illinois

"The Tea Party Express came into town, and I didn't even notice who spoke, because Lana was one of the organizers. I couldn't see anything but her. That's partly because my periwig had slipped down over one eye, but mostly because it was love at first sight. She taught me to talk dirty instead of quoting scripture during sex. It changed my life."

Lauren L.
Waterville, Maine

"You don't see many Jewish guys at Tea Party events—not that I was really looking for a Jewish guy. I just happened to notice Uri in a costume that was kind of a colonial version of a stormtrooper, if the stormtrooper were a Hasidic Jew. I'd never seen anything like it. His protest sign looked like a prologue from a *Star Wars* movie, like, 'A long time ago, in a colony far away...' and then it had some Hebrew from the Old Testament, about the King of Sodom and taxes? Honestly, I was too distracted by the provocative bulge in his costume to make sense of it all. I remember thinking, this guy is special. He bought me a Princess Leia bikini and a shpitzel. We've been together ever since."

Beth S.
Portland, Oregon

"I have family in Kansas, and when I was back for the holidays, there was a rally at the state capitol building. I saw Joren across the square, making a huge ice sculpture of the Boston Tea Party. He'd done the rough outline with an adze and a machete, but now he was working with chisels and bevels and who knows what. I said something about his hand tools. He said he'd made the tools himself. I asked if he'd made the tool-making tools, too—like, just how obsessive are you, was my question. When he looked up, something clicked. The next thing I knew, we were in the shrubbery. We try to stay in touch, but the long-distance thing is iffy. He says he's making a canoe and is going to paddle it all the way across the country to me. But even if I never see him again, we'll always have Topeka."

As those last two anecdotes suggest, creativity is a big draw for Tea Party women. Men who hope to get lucky just by wearing an American flag codpiece should rethink their mating strategies. Don't be afraid to stand out from the crowd. Ben Franklin flew kites in thunderstorms, and Patrick Henry was the Jim DeMint of his day, taking extreme stands and making an ass of himself. Those guys got laid all the time, and apparently (despite being a total homophobe) Sen. DeMint does, too—the sheep of South Carolina say he's not ba-a-a-ad, ha ha.

LOOKING FOR LOVE IN ALL THE RIGHT-WING PLACES

We need more sex appeal on the right. The left has worked tirelessly to attract young people with its "anything-goes" morality. Three of the defining presidencies of the twentieth century (FDR, JFK, and WJC) were Democratic administrations rife with sex. Those three dirty socialists managed staggering numbers of sexual conquests amid challenging national crises (Great Depression, Cold War and civil rights upheavals, economic recession and impeachment). And they did it despite crippling disabilities.

Franklin D. Roosevelt

Wheelchair-bound philanderer Franklin D. Roosevelt married his cousin and had long-term affairs with at least two other women, probably more (let's call it an even thousand). He was reelected three times, and unsubstantiated surveys show that by his fourth term in office, 55 percent of Americans approved of FDR's diddling on the job.

John F. Kennedy

John F. Kennedy ignored painful war injuries to satisfy his legendary sex drive, about which he was known to say, "If I don't shuck the clam at least twice a day, I'll go insane like the rest of my family." First Lady Jackie Kennedy could only handle half that load, so JFK's press secretary, Pamela Turnure (a Jackie look-alike), was assigned to tend his prodigious libido, a task she often outsourced to actresses like Marilyn Monroe and Marlene Dietrich, or to Mafia gun moll Judy Campbell. The press, grateful for sloppy seconds with Ms. Turnure, kept quiet about JFK's dalliances. Only years later can we look back on his sexual incontinence with the objective envy and disgust it deserves.

William Jefferson Clinton

And then there's Bill Clinton, crippled by testosterone itself. The "humper from Hope" would bang anything that looked even vaguely human, including Monica Lewinsky and a cardboard movie-theater standee of Arnold Schwarzenegger, which was later presented to Clinton by his cabinet after he survived impeachment—for obstruction of justice pursuant to a sloppy blowjob. Slick Willie and his staff left a trail of DNA and hush-money payoffs during his two presidential campaigns, and created a pervasive sex-lair atmosphere in the White House. It's estimated that by the year 2000, the Clinton administration had slept with one out of every two people in America.[1]

---

1 TeaBastard.com poll, November 2000, margin of error ±50 percent.

These three Democrats alone account for more than 75 percent of the sex that has taken place in Washington, D.C., over the past eighty years.[2] Republicans have struggled to make their marks—namely, Mark Foley and Mark Sanford. The former fooled around with male House pages and the latter fell deeply, extra-maritally in love and wandered off to South America on the Appalachian Trail or however that geography worked. Senators Larry "wide stance" Craig, John "shtup a staffer's wife" Ensign, and Rep. Chris "no shirtee" Lee tried hard to sex up GOP politics. Philip Giordano even went after pre-teen girls, which this book sweatily condemns. Guys like Newt and Rudy had notable philanderings, but are now obscured by masseuse-seducing Al Gore, and Anthony's Weiner. Senator Dan Burton beat John Edwards to the child-out-of-wedlock punch, but even Arnold's Sperminator act couldn't top cheating on a dying wife. Congressman Ed Schrock joined a long line of anti-gay conservatives who turned out to be queer as a two-dollar liberal.

All we really get from this stuff is a reputation for hypocrisy. For the most part, conservatives, with our alleged family values, haven't been able to compete with liberals. Our moral failings are just as egregious, it seems, but we don't get credit from sex-issues voters for being open-minded. It's up to the Tea Party to bring Real American balls to conservatism.

---

2 *TeaBastard Research Institute study, "Eighty Years of Beltway Boffing" (2011).*

We've got to yank the belt off the Beltway, strip the government bare-naked, and rock the public interest all night long.

GETTING TO YES, YES, OH GOD YES

Sometimes it's hard to hook up at a rally, even though you're crowded together and you know you have a lot in common. Don't make it look like you're only there to get married and laid. Keep some conversation starters handy. If you find a hot prospect only to draw a blank on what to say, try one of these proven ice-breakers:

➡ **"Wanna help me clean my gun?"** This works even better for women trying to pick up men than vice-versa, but if you see a particularly slutty-looking Teababe, you might try tugging at your crotch as you say it.

➡ **"Can I buy you a funnel cake?"** The carnival atmosphere of a Tea Party can be enhanced by the aroma of sweet, greasy dough—and that doesn't always refer to the sweaty, bloated flesh of protesters. If your rally doesn't have a funnel cake stand, consider setting up a deep fryer. You'll make money, meet people, and defy Big Government's oppressive dietary recommendations, all in one fell goop.

➡ **"Know what would look good on you? A bonnet!"** A classic switcheroo. She thinks you're going to say, "Me!" When you say, "A bonnet!" instead, she sees that you're not just another Tea Party player trying to get into her corset, but a classy guy who respects women enough to have them look dowdy. If you actually hand her a bonnet and she accepts it, she kinda owes you.

➟ **"Did you know that surveys show conservatives have better sex lives than liberals?"** If this piques the interest of the person you're hitting on, you can add something like, "Of course, my previous partners probably skewed the results."

➟ **"How do you spell 'fellatio'?"** Great for a woman to use while making a protest sign. You kneel beside your sign on the ground, see, with a marker at the ready. You've already written "Don't shove your engorged taxes down my throat! If Obama wants [blank space here], let Michelle do it!" When a good-looking guy walks by, ask this question in a kind of ditzy, Christine O'Donnell voice. If he actually spells it right, he's probably not your guy. If he looks blank and asks, "What's fellatio?"—well, you're already kneeling. Invite him to pray with you.

TERMS, TECHNIQUES, AND TITILLATING TRENDS

So you snare a potential mate. Now what? Share your beliefs and get your prejudices confirmed? That's all fine, but if you can't follow up the heart-to-heart with some decent hip-to-hip, your partner may lose interest. The downside to the innocence of many Real Americans is that we can be bumbling in the boudoir. Some Tea Party people have never seen an anatomical diagram of the opposite sex, much less a real naked person. They have no idea what's going on Down There. That can be charming at first, but sexual incompetence doesn't wear well. You don't want your lover wandering off in pursuit of happenis, unless you're one of Glenn Beck's wives.

Right-wing heteros don't really understand homosexuality or fetishes or anything out there in libido's left field. Tea Party no likey the gay, but we're being forced into an increasingly tolerant posture as more conservatives come out. It's a slippery slope—partly because of all that lube—and we don't ever want to suggest that the 10 percent sexual minority is equal to the 90 percent majority. America was founded as a Christian, heterosexual nation (according to many Christian heterosexuals).

On the other hand, conservatives don't want to come off as stodgy ol' prudes. And trying new things to keep our marriages lively never hurts—or maybe it does, a little! The following glossary of kinks and catchy sex jargon will help keep you abreast of trends in political perversion.

ASS-POUNDING: (1) rough anal sex, or (2) a brutal GOP victory over Democrats—euphemized as a "shellacking" after the 2010 mid-terms

ATM: a porn-industry abbreviation for "ass-to-mouth," but never mind, you don't want to think about this every time you withdraw cash, which should be a sacred experience

BACHMAKKAKE: the circle jerk that serves as a benediction to all gatherings of the Tea Party Caucus

BIZZLE MY JIZZLE: street-code for sex between a lobbyist and a congressional aide

BOEHNER: a condition caused by masturbating while eating Cheetos; see **orangina**

CORNHOLE: formerly a euphemism for anal sex, this now refers to a politician who accepts sexual favors from agribusiness or the ethanol lobby

CUNNILINGUS: the disgusting act of oral sex on a woman, which Real Americans eschew

DIRTY SANFORD: like a dirty Sanchez (don't ask), but performed out of love, not lust

DOUBLE DILDO: a sex party with California senators Barbara Boxer and Dianne Feinstein—once a hot fund-raising ticket, before they became hundreds of years old

ELECTING THE PRESIDENT: male masturbation; also known as **caucusing** or simply **voting**

FACE THE NATION: see **cunnilingus**

FELLATIO PRO QUO: the beautiful act of oral sex on a man in exchange for a political favor

GOVERNMENT SPENDING: slang for compulsive promiscuity

HAMBONE: Jew-on-Protestant sex, e.g., Al Franken boning Sen. John Thune

ICE-CUBE SANDWICH: putting ice in the rectum to heighten sensation, or to warm it up gradually after being literally cold-cocked by Dick Cheney

JOINT SESSION OF CONGRESS: bipartisan fuck-buddies, e.g., John Thune boning Al Franken

LEGISLATION: sodomy

MAMIE & DWIGHT: vaginal insertion of an entire bald head

MEET THE PRESS: a return to partisan bickering after a **joint session of Congress**

MONICORONA: any sexual practice involving cigars

N.E.A. GRANT: talking dirty while sexually desecrating a national monument

ORANGINA: the female version of a **boehner**

PAUL'S LETTERS TO THE EPHESIANS: sex in the National Cathedral during a filibuster

PUSHING THE BILL THROUGH COMMITTEE: pooping on a partner

QUEERJET: homosexual act aboard Air Force One (Democratic administration only)

ROMNEYCARE: sex with a plastic mannequin or EPA crash-test dummy

SENATOR INHOFE: regret-inducing sex with a complete idiot

SMOOT-HAWLEY: pushing an erection down and turning it to point backwards

TEABAGGING: a noble, balls-in-your-face practice of our well-hung founding fathers

TOMB OF THE UNKNOWN FUCKTARD: sex closet in the office of the minority whip

UNITED NATIONS SECURITY COUNCIL: group sex with foreign diplomats

VISIT WITH HEADS OF STATE: oral sex between allegedly heterosexual men

WIKILEAK: a populist campaign fundraiser in which candidates allow constituents to pee on them in exchange for donations; formerly called a **pisslestop**

YOUNG REPUBLICAN CONVENTION: a botched orgy resulting in widespread blueballs

This is not an exhaustive list, and liberal readers will be yawning by now, as every Democratic administration has encouraged such activities. But less corrupted conservatives may be shocked—and still confused about how to proceed with a Tea Party hook-up. What do you do, once you've met the Real American of your dreams? How do you keep him or her satisfied? To help lube the pistons of the Republic, *The Tea Party Guide* hereby presents a few basic sexual positions from an obscure pamphlet called *The Right Way to Do It*, more commonly referred to as the *Tea Party Kama Sutra*. (WARNING: This is sinful, pornographic, and there's not enough of it.)

The original *Kama Sutra* is, obviously, for sexually advanced foreigners. It requires years

"Congress of the Baboons," from the original *Kama Sutra*.

of developing flexibility and stamina through the practice of yoga, an evil art of the exotic East, to do stuff like that. And apparently it requires the man to wear a dress and dye his junk with henna. *The Tea Party Kama Sutra* advises you to keep it simple and, with no filthy illustrations to help, suggests that you base most of your deviant dirtiness on the missionary position, which, after all, is totally Christian. Variations include:

The Tiger Mother at Rest
This position is especially good for busy parents, when the woman is too exhausted to fully participate after a day of yelling at children, and the man requires release of pent-up anger at sexual deprivation and government policy. The woman lies on her back and falls asleep as the man climaxes prematurely at the mere prospect of sex.

Ronnie & Mommy
This popular position is a tribute to the Reagans, with the man wobbling his head between the thighs of the woman and murmuring delusional anecdotes of World War II as she receives an astrology reading (variation: manicure). NOTE: This is as close to cunnilingus AND a Satanic three-way as conservatives should ever get.

The Subcommittee on Net Neutrality
With the woman supine and holding a laptop computer over her face, the man thrusts distractedly while blogging or checking email.

Kneading the Loaf

This is sometimes the only position possible if both partners are morbidly obese. The man first rolls the woman in flour so that he can find the wet spot. She then positions her hips at the edge of the bed or dining room table, so the man may hoist his gut up to rest on top of hers and, if he is lucky, achieve penetration. His hands are free in this position, so it is advised to keep a box of Krispy Kremes or other snacks nearby.

The Rage of the Silver Fox

An expressive outlet for her frustration if he is unable to perform, this is a daring "woman astride" position, with the man in the customary supine-female posture. She kneels over him, holding his member like a microphone and shouting angrily as if giving an impromptu speech at a Tea Party rally, occasionally tapping the glans with her other hand and yelling, "Is this thing on?"

HAPPY ENDING

Other positions in the *Tea Party Kama Sutra* may require more flexibility and strength, but most were designed with the armchair politico in mind. Remember, sex isn't so much about technique as it is about enthusiasm and making use of our God-given testosterone and political anger. Pour that energy like salad dressing onto every fresh romantic encounter with fellow Real Americans. And then toss that salad.

Who knows, you might find more than just a casual hook-up. You might find a soul (if any) mate. If you're like other satisfied Tea Party patriots, that discovery may lead to the ultimate conservative value: family. When it does, you'll want to raise those Real Little Americans extremely right. The next chapter will show you how.

CHAPTER EIGHT

TRAINING TOMORROW'S TEABAGGERS TODAY

TEABAGGERS ARE THE OPPOSITE of poets: they're made, not born. Sure, there may be a genetic predisposition toward anti-government sentiment, conspiracy theories, and misspelled protest signs, but we can't depend on even the shallowest gene pool to do all the work in producing junior members of the Tea Party. That's like asking our ancestors for a handout. We have to work to put the fear of God and hatred of liberals into kids.

NATURE VS. NURTURE VS. NIETZSCHE

Nothing less than the future of humanity is at stake. That's why it's important to drop the name "Nietzsche" (pronounced "knee-tzsche") right up front here, because it sounds impressive, like we've really thought this out. Nietzsche was the German guy who said, "God is dead," which is a terrible thing to say, and if he were still around, we'd try to link him to

Acorn and the Rev. Jeremiah Wright. What Nietzsche meant is that most parents and children no longer get their values from God or even from talk radio. Without the right values, what do we get? A socialist from Kenya as the president of the United States, and a Real American like Tom DeLay being forced to dance for money or be some brutal felon's bitch.

In a secular age, where do values come from? This is where Nietzsche's other famous idea raises its big ol' head: the theory of the Superman, or *Übermensch*. The theory is that humanity must find a heroic revolutionary, a Superman who can inspire us to greatness and see through walls and bend steel with his bare hands.

Beck, der Übermensch.

For the Tea Party, this hero is Glenn Beck, the potato-headed pundit who kicked off the movement with his "9/12 Project," calling us to return to the spirit that united America in the aftermath of whatever that thing was that happened on 9/11 that one time.

THE MAKING OF AN ÜBERMENSCH

Descended from humble German immigrants, Glenn Beck overcame both their humility and their ethnicity to surpass

Rush Limbaugh in Real American pandering and ego-bloat. But it was a long road getting to where he is today. Bullied as a child, frightened of books, cursed with ADHD—hey what's that over there—Beck never really fit in. Like most dumpy outcasts, he initially used alcohol and drugs to transcend his lowly lot in life, but soon discovered that broadcasting was far more effective and addictive. His early forays into radio were largely uneventful, with occasional flashes of greatness, such as his open mockery of minorities. But it was a prank call to the wife of a rival radio host, during which Beck made fun of the woman's recent miscarriage, that taught him the power of the medium.

"Talk radio is like sex," said Beck, in a recent fake interview. "It's fast-paced and women get upset."

Like Sean Hannity, an ex-boyfriend from his experimental adolescence, Beck is a high school-educated bloviator who came to conservatism via the usual route: a childlike ignorance of politics, government, history, or logic. Naturally, Fox gave him a TV show.[1]

"My opinions were always way stronger than my knowledge," Beck boasts, "just like Keith Olbermann's breath is way stronger than his ratings."

Beck sired dozens of children during his wild youth, but never had the chance to inculcate them with conservative values, a regret he calls "haunting—although I don't really

---

1 *At press time, his show had just been canceled. Like the Lord it claims to speak for, Fox giveth and taketh away. (—ed.)*

remember having kids back then." This claim is uncharacteristically believable, as the 1980s and 1990s were a period of heavy drinking and drug use for Beck, culminating in a DUI arrest that was the catalyst for his conversion to Mormonism during a prison Bible study and gang rape.

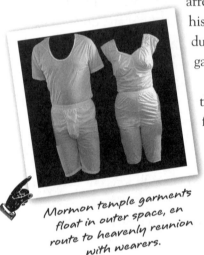

Mormon temple garments float in outer space, en route to heavenly reunion with wearers.

"We Mormons believe that our salvation lies in family," Beck explains, "and that we will be reunited in heaven, complete with our special underwear."

Does this concept include the women and children from yesteryear's trysts as well, or only his current family? On this point, Beck is surprisingly humble. "I don't presume to know God's mind," he says, "but He would never let my ex-wives into heaven, because they're all notorious Catholics and non-denominational whatever. Also, some of them lie about how much back child support I owe."

This deeply spiritual Superman often reflects on the lost opportunity to raise all his offspring, as well as his audience, in the manner he prescribes for America.

"If I'd had a few years with all those kids, they'd now be stay-at-home moms and hard-working dads, home-schooling

Teabaggers of their own, and making hysterical, paranoid calls to my program," Beck chokes wistfully, "but I hear some of them think for themselves, like the godless whores from whence they issued. Whoa, did I just say, 'from whence'? Well, listen to fancy elitist me!" Self-awareness is not the usual métier of this media titan, but glimpses of sentience do occasionally peek through.

APPLYING THE PRINCIPLES LIKE A PATRIOTIC POULTICE

The Übermensch approach to child-rearing got its first serious tryout with Beck's eighth marriage. After learning of a daycare center that played his radio show all day for its young charges, Beck adopted the thirty-five preschoolers, two comely daycare workers, and the center's clueless program director. In a gesture that some describe as "magnanimous to the point of kidnapping," Beck had them all carted by shipping container across the country to his family compound in Connecticut. The thirty-five new members of Beck's vast clan are kept in a Skinner box (the shipping container, outfitted with a plexiglass window and corner toilet) wallpapered with images of America's greatness. Imagine growing up surrounded by inspirational posters of founding father and slave-boinker Thomas Jefferson, anti-communist and vicious drunk Joe McCarthy, and your own famous patriarch in a unitard, cape, and singlet. That's the sweet life for Beck's tribe.

"I work a lot, so I don't have much time with the fam,"

Beck concedes. "But they still get to see and hear me every day. I'm also a famous indie musician, with platinum-selling albums such as *Odelay* and *Midnite Vultures* to my credit, and the kids' room is wired for every concert, radio and TV show, audiobook, ringtone, and Rally to Restore Honor, so they can never escape my voice, my face…my heart." (The Beck family Skinner box also features a photo of Dad's heart, taken during a recent medical procedure.)

The discovery that he could run his family strictly and narcissistically, yet remotely, led Beck to believe anyone could raise a right-wing extremist, and compelled him to share his unique parenting methods with the world. They are the basis for much of what follows, and are fully vetted by Sarah Palin, who threw in her two cents' worth for a nominal, six-figure consulting fee.

Do these methods work? Beck's wives seem to think so.

"My wife seems to think so," says Beck, "but like I said, I'm a busy guy, so I wouldn't know. I'm currently working on Volume Two of my poignant memoir, *The Christmas Sweater*. It's all about how I sweat a lot at Christmas. Anyway, I'm busy."

UNHELPFUL SUBHEAD

That's the beauty of raising Teabaggers. It's as much about what you don't do as what you do, and more about what you don't know than what you know. It's about ethics and science, and how to ignore and discredit these things. It's about our children—and our children's children, because even a child can raise children using these methods.

But we must be vigilant. Corrupting influences are everywhere, and the best-intentioned, least-educated, lily-white Midwesterners can end up raising a dreadlocked grad student who ruins every Thanksgiving dinner by whining about global warming and social justice. Only a combination of the right parenting, the right Bible-enriched school curricula, and the right (-wing) media influences can prevent this. It's up to all of us to create the Tea Party's next generation and instill our beliefs in them before dirty liberal influences brainwash them.

LET'S PLAY CELEBRITY SIDEBAR!

Why does the left get almost all the celebrities? Is it just that celebrities are so often gay, and find a more welcoming atmosphere among dirty socialists? Or is there something in liberalism that's inherently attractive to the artistically inclined? If so, what is it? And where can the Tea Party get some of it? Because if there's one thing liberals have going for them, it's celebrity support—and that affects kids, who tend to be influenced less by their hideous parents than by actors, movie stars, and other communists. That's not to say there are no celeb-righties. But just look at all these ce-left-brities:

- ⇒ Oprah
- ⇒ Sean Penn
- ⇒ Susan Sarandon
- ⇒ Alec Baldwin
- ⇒ Meryl Streep
- ⇒ George Clooney
- ⇒ Brangelina
- ⇒ Bruce Springsteen

- Sting
- Bono
- Madonna
- Cher
- Moby (almost anyone with one name)
- Woody Allen
- Woody Harrelson (almost any Woody)
- Don Cheadle
- Dustin Hoffman
- Ed Asner
- Jessica Lange
- Spike Lee
- Oliver Stone
- Rob Reiner
- Jon Stewart
- Janeane Garofalo
- Ben Affleck
- Matt Damon
- Jimmy Buffett
- Jane Fonda
- Whoopi Goldberg
- Warren Beatty
- Shirley MacLaine
- Debra Winger
- Robert Redford
- Paul Newman (still selling health food posthumously)
- Viggo Mortensen
- Martin Sheen
- Bradley Whitford
- Cameron Diaz
- Roger Ebert
- Ashton Kutcher
- The Dixie Chicks
- Kanye West
- P. Diddy
- Bonnie Raitt
- REM
- Pearl Jam
- Lenny Kravitz
- Dave Matthews Band
- Radiohead
- Green Day
- Lady Gaga
- Peter Gabriel
- Stevie Wonder
- Joan Baez
- Don Henley
- James Taylor
- and of course, Barbra Streisand

Who's on the right? The Tea Party has found it hard to attract the pretty people. Oh, we've had Trace Adkins and Richard Petty and a few other country stars and NASCAR drivers show up at rallies, but who's really using the bully pulpit of fame on behalf of Real Americans? If we expand "the right" to mean registered Republicans, professed libertarians, and people who say things like, "I think we should just trust the president in every decision that he makes" (during a George W. Bush presidency, no less) the list may not be Tea Party central, but the right can claim a few major celebs:

Arnold

Clint

Chuck

Jessica

Britney

Heather

Mel

Charlton

Hey, hold on. Look at that list. It's a big, delicious, blonde-bombshell burger, with Britney Spears, Heather Locklear, and Jessica Simpson as the meat, an ass-kicking top bun of Arnold Schwarzenegger, Clint Eastwood, and Chuck Norris, and a slightly thinner, ethnic-slurring, gun-toting bottom bun of Mel Gibson and Charlton Heston. Wait, that makes the bottom of the bun cold and dead. Let's trade Heston for…

The Rock

Yep, Dwayne Johnson, the handsomest, charmingest, bad-assest wrestler/actor/Rock ever, is a registered Republican. So is Kid Rock, but nobody needs to see that.

We also have Dennis Miller and Drew Carey. Admittedly, neither of those guys is very funny anymore, but if it's comedy you want, we've got Dr. Phil (ha-ha, Oprah!). And, of course, we've got Ted Nugent. Throw in Bo Derek and Susan Lucci and a few other D-listers and it starts looking better. None of these people will ever show up at a Greenpeace gathering or Sierra Club meeting. They'll never lend their star power to some environmental cause that's going to put a hitch in the get-along of American industry. With their help, the enviro-Nazi Hollywood left is beginning to lose its grip on this country.

RIGHT, WRITER, RE-WRITEST

Of course, the left also claims the lion's share of writers, poets, photographers, painters, dancers, and many of the trade union members in film and music. Except for country & western, the liberal edge in musicians is staggering, especially among singer-songwriters. We've got to work on developing musical talent among Teabaggers, which is hard when you're trying to slash funding for the arts in schools, but that's just a tightrope we're going to have to walk. Imagine if we'd had Woody Guthrie on *our* side:

> This land is your land
> But mostly my land
> Fuck California
> Frack the New York islands
> Chop the redwood forests
> Oil the Gulf Stream waters
> This land was made for mostly me

Or just think if that pot-smokin' Marxist, John Lennon, had gotten his mind right:

> Imagine there's no lefties
> It's easy if you try
> No regulations
> To suck the profits from your environment-
> ravaging industry dry

Imagine all the people, listening to a right-wing Bono:

> I want a gun
> I want to hate
> I wanna tear down the wall
> Between church and state
> I wanna reach out
> And drill, baby, drill
> Where the seas have no spill…

Feel that surge of patriotism? Music hits on an emotional level in people, so you can win hearts and minds without having to argue kids out of their stupid cherished beliefs.

GROWING-UP-EXTREMELY-RIGHT PRINCIPLES FOR TEABAGGERS

So how do we raise right children who live amongst so much wrong? By applying the "Growing-Up-Extremely-Right Principles" that Glenn Beck developed in his own backyard—technically, his garage—and making sure our kids know who's boss: God. And us parents. And also Glenn Beck. You'll recognize a few of these Principles from previous chapters, because they're not just for raising kids; they're also for keeping Teabaggers on the straight and narrow. So we copped a few ideas from the list and padded the book with them. Don't tell the editor.

Read on to learn these powerful Principles. Or just "know"

them without bothering to read, because in your heart, if any, you already know the truths in this book. The liberal media will say you never read, anyway. They don't understand how serious this movement is. They think we're going to rallies dressed up like John Adams and Dolly Madison and a Hitlerized Obama just for fun. They'd better get a clue, because we're not playing around. We're revolting.

The Principles

Think of this list like the Ten Commandments. It should be carved in stone in the lobby of every government building, daycare center, school, church, and home in America. If we all follow these Principles, kids will grow up knowing who to obey, how to behave, what talking points to parrot, and where to aim their guns when the perennial Shiite hits the proverbial fatwa, whatever that means. Read 'em, teach 'em, live 'em:

1. America is good. Everything else is bad. (If I've been paying attention, I already know this. If I haven't, I should re-skim Chapter 1.)

2. God is the awesomest guy ever. He is the boss, and if He commands me to knife my kid, I'm not going to wuss out at the last second and pretend that He changed His mind, like that pansy-Jew Abraham did. God doesn't change His mind! And He doesn't tell you to do something crazy and then go, "Psych! Just testing you!" God works in mysterious ways, not stupid ways. I mean, come on.

3. Aside from that, the Bible's ironclad. I must take it literally and shut the hell up.

4. I must take personal responsibility, if I can't find anyone else to take it first.

5. When Jesus wrote the Constitution, he did not intend for us to dick around with it. All good laws are based on it, and when we break them, we break Jesus' heart. Is that what you want, kid? Of course not. BUT! Bad laws, like gun control, come from Satan and his socialist minions. God wants us to break these laws. Well, maybe not break, but bend and complain about them loudly. It is not un-American for me to disagree with authority, unless I'm challenging the word of God as expressed by a Real American, in which case I should be shot.

6. I must strive to be a more honest person than I was yesterday. Yesterday, I lied like a freakin' Clinton.

7. Sex is evil, especially if I really know what I'm doing or if I'm a woman.

8. The family is sacred. Even the Obama family, we have to admit, is pretty good, considering they're not actually Americans.

9. Consistency is crucial. Don't say one thing and do another when kids are around. If kids call me on my hypocrisy, I've got to shut that down, pronto. I can either deny the contradiction or embrace it, explaining that it's too complicated for kids to grasp—and then slap 'em around for pointing it out. Kids exist to serve parents, teachers, ministers, corporate masters, and the

country at large. Let them start thinking for themselves, and we're screwed.

10. Stay in school—preferably, at home. But don't stay too long. And forget college. Like I'm going to pay that kind of money just so you can forsake these principles and start asking questions I can't answer? Fat chance, smarty-pants.

How do these Principles apply in real life? Let's do some role-playing and find out. You play the part of the child, and this book will play the part of the parent, teaching you a thing or two. We'll call this book "Christine O'Donnell," a Tea Party favorite who has no kids but certainly has a lot of opinions about how to raise them.

In this role-playing scene, Christine O'Donnell catches you masturbating in your room and applies Principle #7. So please get in character and begin rubbing one out.

YOU: Mmmm. Oh, yeah….mmmm….

CHRISTINE O'DONNELL: Hi there, sinner!

YOU: Jeez! Don't you knock?! Who *are* you?

CO'D: I knocked, but I guess it wasn't loud enough to be heard over the buzz of your butt-plug! Don't get up. Just wallow there in sinful lust, abusing your body for non-procreative purposes. I'm Christine O'Donnell, and I went broke running for the U.S. Senate in the state of Delaware. Would you like to help defray my campaign costs?

YOU: Will you leave if I do?

CO'D: A big donation would send me straight to the bank, because I'm in financial trouble. Apparently, I evaded income tax and used campaign funds to pay my rent.

YOU: If I give you enough money, will you have sex with me?

CO'D: No! Sex is evil, especially if you know what you're doing, and I learned quite a bit in college! Besides, I'm supposed to be playing the part of the parent in this scene. Having sex with you would be incest, which may be even worse than masturbation.

YOU: Well, I guess you don't really want the money, then.

CO'D: Okay, okay, I'll have sex with you!

Aaaaand, Scene! Well, that didn't go as planned. You kids these days are so hard to raise extremely right! But at least Christine O'Donnell managed to stop you from masturbating, which is very important to her and to the Tea Party. As we learned in the previous chapter, only in marriage can sex create the Real Americans of tomorrow. And remember, marriage is between one man and one woman. Except in the case of Glenn Beck—he's too much man for one woman.

BE FLEXIBLE (NOT REALLY)

These Principles can save families from a lot of heartaches (and headaches—you'll never have to think again!) if you ditch political correctness and pack some parental punch. Let's say one of your kids decides to believe in the theory of evolution. You can hit that with Principle #3: the Bible is ironclad. If a little forced reading of Genesis doesn't work, try beating the science right out of the child, explaining that "adaptation through 'survival of the fittest' hurts me more than it hurts you." Just watch how fast your young Darwinian drops that "hot mutato" and picks up an "irreducibly complex" eyeball instead—especially if you've knocked it out of the socket.

Likewise, if a child believes government can solve problems, refer to Principle #4 and insist on personal responsibility. But be ready to improvise. Let's say a demented grandparent praises Medicare, and your kid finds out that this government-run health plan gives our most expensive patients—the elderly—coverage that's cheaper than private insurance. This idea is like a gateway drug that could cause a child to embrace Obamacare. Better move fast! First, yell "Socialism!" and point, distracting the kid. Next, discredit grandma or grandpa, suggesting that Medicare causes brain damage. Lastly, hire a faceless government bureaucrat to show up at the pediatrician's office, literally standing between your child and his or her doctor. Children find faceless people terrifying, so this should drive the point home. If not, again, beating usually works.

OFFER VOID IN ALASKA

The Palin family is a great example of how strict parental adherence to a right-wing ethos can win minds and influence children. You may recall that during the 2008 election, Sarah

The Überwomensch breastfeeds two marmots while delivering an inspiring speech.

Palin's multiple roles as governor of Alaska, mayor of Wasilla, and mother to scads of quirkily named children astounded many Americans. With goldbricker First Laddie, Todd, gone dog-sledding and snowmobiling for days on end, where did she get the time, they asked? What did she do to stay so peppy and perky, they wondered? How did she do it all with no sign of ever having learned anything, they inquired? Since then, she's added bestselling author, Fox News "journalist," reality show star, and top-ten Twitterista to her long list of overachievements. Liberal pundits have mocked each of these in turn, failing to note her integration of them all into a kind of executive Superwoman role. The *Überwomensch*. Remember how deftly the Überwomensch handled the press when daughter Bristol's teen pregnancy threatened to derail Sarah's candidacy? She attacked the media like a true Mama Grizzly for dragging her family into the spotlight, even as she nailed the kids' feet to the spotlit spot on the floor to boost her credibility as a family-values candidate? Remember when Katie Couric sandbagged her with gotcha-journalism questions like, "What news publications do you read?" Remember how nonchalantly Sarah dismissed that question, along with the follow-ups that revealed her inability to name a single publication she'd ever laid eyes on? Remember how the lamestream media pounced on that as evidence of her lack of knowledge or interest in world affairs, and how only the enrightened among us understood her as a Real American, a woman who simply *knows* without having to stoop to "learning"?

She knows that true freedom means being able to retrofit facts to support pre-existing beliefs, such as her 2011 assertion that the Soviet Union won the space race, but the cost of it destroyed the country. She didn't need to understand that neither of those things were true. Her belief is that government spending is bad, period. That's all we need to know. Who cares if she used more federal aid as governor of Alaska than any other governor in the country? So what if state government spending increased by nearly a third when she was at the helm? Who cares if she hired lobbyists to bring home $25 million in federal pork when she was mayor of Wasilla, a town of 7,000?

The point is that she has principles, not that she contradicts them. In fact, you can't contradict your own principles if you don't have them in the first place. (Don't think about that one too long—it hurts.) Besides, it's Sarah Palin's prerogative as a woman to change her mind, right? Like a true Queen Mama Grizzly, she supported Bristol's pregnancy with state-funded health care after cutting unwed mothers' social services in Alaska. In the wild, a mother grizzly will feed another bear's cubs to her own, if food is scarce enough. To defend her own wayward offspring, she'd maul Levi Johnston to an unrecognizable pile of viscera—which this book would pay to see.

Critics may carp that a "family values" political candidate should have known what her teenage daughter's vagina was up to and maybe chaperoned Bristol's dates or slapped on a chastity belt. Some have gone so far as to say that the Palins clearly didn't raise the girl extremely right. But anyone who watched Bristol cavort on *Dancing with the Stars* knows that she was raised to display a sense of confidence that's disproportionate to her abilities and to take full advantage of her fame to grub for money. That's the good, capitalist, Christian influence of her parents on display. As a former beauty pageant contestant, Sarah knows how to work a dim-witted crowd, and she passed that talent on to her daughters. Middle child, Willow, has already shown a gift for grabbing headlines by cussing up a storm on her Facebook page. The Palin kids are self-starters. Who wouldn't be, with a mom like that?

Sarah Palin's integrity is at such a high level, most of us can't even comprehend it, especially since she herself apparently doesn't. She's the living embodiment of Raising-Kids-Extremely-Right Principle #9: consistency. She's all about it: consistently free of thoughts, consistently willing to contradict herself, consistently right, right, right.

The Growing-Up-Extremely-Right Principles are yours to use as you see fit, as long as you pay your licensing fees.

This is like donating to Wikipedia, only it supports the Tea Party instead of Democrats and other socialists. Send donations to this book at TeaBastard.com and some of it will probably make its way to Glenn Beck. Freedom ain't free. It takes money and punditry to keep kids safe from actual thought.

And as we head into our final geographic survey of Tea Parties, remember that parents and all Real American grown-ups are like lobbyists, influencing the "swing state" of childhood in the election season of life. Swing it to the right!

CHAPTER NINE

Swingin' to the Right: A State-by-State Guide (Part 3)

THE IMPORTANCE OF THIS chapter can't be overstated, but here goes. What we do in a swing state echoes in eternity. The Tea Parties here are the most important Tea Parties ever, except MAYBE the original Boston one. These crucial events can turn the tide for Real Americans across the country, even in landlocked states that have no tide, because this is where the Teabags are in hot water, so to speak. These states make or break conservative rule of America. Are you getting this? Are you packing the car or booking flights yet? If not, you just sentenced your country to four more years of hard socialism.

Way to go.

COLORADO

State Fear: Without mountains, we'd be Kansas
State Price Gouger: Whole Foods
State Tax Revenue Boost: Medicinal marijuana, man

All About Colorado

The Rocky Mountains gazing down over the countercultural mecca of Boulder seem to smile at its hippie-dippie denizens as if to say, hey…got glaucoma? And they do: since this state cleared the way for medicinal marijuana, the economy has popped like a sensimilla seed in a chamber pipe. The stoner strain in the Coloradoan personality seems to be coexisting just fine with the traditional redneck survivalist strain. Must be all those Coexist bumpstickers. Anyway, there's a lot of freedom here. Come get some.

August is *Thin Air Month!*

This celebration of the already difficult-to-breathe air in the Mile-High State welcomes motorcycles, lawn mowers, Hummers, and all other manner of combustible enginery to "combust up the joint"! Tires are burned nightly, and as a special treat, even the youngest children are encouraged to smoke like chimneys. Which are also encouraged to smoke.

FLORIDA
State Visual Metaphor: Penis
State Chad: Hangin'
State Jeb: Bush

All About Florida

There was a time when Tea Party values couldn't have made a dent in this weird, Jewspanic state. And then came Marco Rubio, trailing clouds of glory (see Chapter 11 for bold predictions about his political future). Still, you can't expect a place that's been sugarcane-holed from top to bottom to function like a real state. From Ponce de Leon to all the fountain-of-douche seekers thereafter, it's been like a big toxic playpen for every land speculator, shyster lawyer, Zionist floozy, suntan broker, and fugitive from ethnographic justice who ever wanted to go somewhere really humid. Besides rigging elections badly, there's not much Real American stuff here. But try this:

¡Hasta Luego, Cubanos!

This lighthearted annual attempt to convince all of them to go back is fun for the whole family, unless it's a Cuban family. But they should go back, you know. All of them. Even the really hot, salsa-dancing ones. They're only stealing jobs from chubby white people with no sense of rhythm.

IOWA

State Fuzzy Distinction: Caucuses and Caucasians

State Great Folk Song About the Early '60s: Greg Brown's "Brand New '64 Dodge"

State Cob: Corn

All About Iowa

Iowa is conflicted. Easily influenced, yet stubbornly aphasic, it doesn't know whether it wants to be a beacon of freedom or a handmaiden to tyranny, and isn't quite sure which is which. Catching liberal germs from Minnesota during the Bush years, Iowa jump-started Obama's campaign in the caucuses and legalized gay marriage, a one-two punch that had conservatives doubled over, holding their nads and trying not to throw up. Democrats took advantage of that moment to eat all the pie. It's a tricky state, but by pandering to agribusiness and base fears about minorities turning the tables on white folks, Teabaggers can push Iowa back into the red.

Family Farm Fest

October is set aside to honor the farmers who pay substandard wages to unregistered workers. And, of course, people who have the time hang around for November, which is Anti-Immigrant Month. In election years, anyway.

MISSOURI

State Homosexual Panic: What if Iowa makes us gay?

State Riff on *Toy Story*: "There's some meth in mah bootheel!"

State Guy Whose Singing Always Bothered Us: John Ashcroft

State Guy We Hate to Love: Harry Truman

All About Missouri

The borders of this misshapen state were drawn by a drunken governor who bet his poker buddies he could make Missouri touch every other state in the Union. He failed, but Missouri has had its Midwestern mitts on Iowa, Illinois, Kentucky, Kansas, and Nebraska, and has touched Tennessee, Oklahoma, and Arkansas "down there."

Missouri's prescient voting record reliably predicted presidential outcomes for centuries. Then the state went for Adlai Stevenson instead of Eisenhower and had to take a bellwether refresher. It didn't work; they faltered again when they bet on McCain. So they abandoned election-predicting and took up meth-cooking.

The Tea Party here is notoriously tubby, and has submitted a bill to the legislature to change Missouri's nickname from the "Show Me State" to the "Show Me My Feet State."

Show Me the Green Card Time

For one sweaty day each summer, all Missourians in Kansas City's vast suburbs and exurbs trim their own hedges in a moving and powerful demonstration that Americans can get along just fine without any outside-the-borders help for up to an entire day. By evening, they fall exhausted into the strong, brown arms of gardeners and housekeepers. Interracial lovemaking ensues…wait a minute, this isn't a Tea Party! Do NOT go to Show Me The Green Card Time. It's some kind of trick.

Can't You Shut That Kid Up?! Days

The shrieking laughter of children fills the City Museum in St. Louis each spring, as adults try and mostly fail to squelch natural human exuberance. Winners get aspirin.

NEW HAMPSHIRE

State Bird: The Grey-Crested Curmudgeon
State Demonym We're Not Comfortable With: New Hampshrite
State Befuddlement: I thought we were Vermont!

All About New Hampshire

The "Come On, Let's Not Sugar-Coat It" strain in the state's fiercely independent character showed up recently, when a group of New Hampshrites submitted a ballot proposal to change the state slogan from "Live Free Or Die" to "Live Free AND Die." New Hampshire's governor, John Lynch, scuttled the measure, saying, "I know it's true, but it makes my buttocks clench uncomfortably." Wussy Democrats like that give this state its waffliness. New Hampshire needs more tough-talkin' Teabaggers. Jump in.

Olde Hampshire Time
A four-day-long complete and utter rejection of everything that replaced anything that came before it. Formerly, *John Smith Sailed Up Yon Coast That One Time*. Before that, *Hunting, Gathering, and Mate-Dragging Time*.

NEW MEXICO
State Song: "Vaya Con Dios Mio Hay Mexicanos Aquí"
State Alternative Slogan: "Fuck You, Arizona!"
State Pretty Drive: Taos to Eagle's Nest to that one little town that has the cute dealio

All About New Mexico
They tend to elect Republicans to state office and Democrats to national office here, a division that seems to work for New Mexico, but is infuriating to conservatives around the country, who honestly would rather just have this embarrassingly named state go back to where it came from. That doesn't look

likely, with a 44 percent Hispanic population who spent way too much time and energy escaping Old Mexico to ever go back. Ever. Unless we make 'em, which we should. But then who'd do all the work around here?

And Better! Campaign

An annual three-month letter-writing campaign to state and federal officials to get the name changed to New *And Better!* Mexico, just in case that isn't painfully obvious already. Which it totally is. But still.

NEVADA

State Tragic Hero: Moe Green
State Disturbing Trend: Freaky Frenchies from Cirque du Soleil wandering Las Vegas, speaking French and doing parkour and creepy clown crap
State Ranch: Bunny

All About Nevada

Many states around the country are now looking at Nevada's example of economic development and saying, "Hmmm, maybe we should make everything legal, too." The libertarianism of Nevada offers gambling in every form, prostitution in every position and pricing niche, and tickets to more gun shows than a body-building contest. Oh, and steroids are totally cool here. Pseudoephedrine is getting harder to come by, though, so aspiring meth-cookers are advised to stay in Fresno where they belong.

Take Back the Casinos!

A night-long march protesting the tragic mistake that gave Native Americans the right to something. By the way, that thing of saying "Native Americans"? We take that back— they're Indians. From India. They've got call centers; do they really need casinos too? How far will this relentless oppression of Real Americans go? We ask ya.

OHIO

State Cool Name for a Town: Chagrin Falls

State Riddle: "What's hi in the middle and round on the outside? Nope, it's not a boob."

State Ominous Threat: We killed Lake Erie once, and we can do it again

All About Ohio

People are bailing out of Ohio faster than a bucket brigade can clean up a fish kill. The socialist, Big-Brothery U.S. Census has stripped the state of several congressional districts in the past decade, and Ohio's governor has offered every remaining resident a tax-free abandoned factory just to stay put. Now is the time for all good Teabaggers to come to the aid of the Rust Belt. We can beat back the job-killing liberals and replace them with job-discussing conservatives. Maybe sooner or later, there'll be some jobs.

Illegal Nanny Recognition

The best families gather without their nannies to talk about how much they appreciate and enjoy the dedication, ability, and generosity of their illegal nannies. Price fixing for the following year is set at this event and light hors d'oeuvres are served.

Dirty Diebold Days

This election-week festival celebrates the electronic voting machine and its best-known manufacturer. Software hacking contests take place amid "paper trail" confetti and "We'll deliver Ohio to the GOP" streamers that were cut from Diebold executive memos. Souvenir voter cards, $5. Souvenir voter cards authenticated by Black Box Voting as hacked, $100. Funnel cake, $3.

PENNSYLVANIA

State Hobby: Hydraulic fracturing
State Cocktail: The flaming tapwater fizz
State Invidious Comparison: Stupid ol' New York, always lording it over us!
State Crack: The one in the Liberty Bell. Not that stupid ol' cocaine!

All About Pennsylvania

This declining industrial giant was once mostly pristine rolling woodlands. What began as the biggest land-grant ever given to an individual (called "William Penn's morning wood" by snickering colonists back in the day) evolved into a manufacturing titan in the nineteenth century, and then a manufacturing Titanic in the late twentieth. Good times!

The political division in Pennsylvania is between the urban northeast half and the rural/suburban southwest half of the state, with the former voting heavily blue and the latter voting furiously red. The GOP strategy centers on fomenting a culture war between these Fake and Real Americans, and getting CNN commentators to harp on it constantly as correspondent John King dinks around with his computer map on election night. The Democratic strategy, as usual, is non-existent. There's plenty of room for Teabaggers here.

Amish Suspicion Festival

With the Amish's iffy relationship with capitalism, a measurable lack of dependence on oil, and an almost complete disregard for conservative bloggers, this may be the craziest idea for a Tea Party ever. What, exactly, are they up to? How can it hurt us? How can we profit from it? Let's have some of this weird but delicious pie and ponder.

★★★

Now that we've surveyed the red, blue, swingin' entirety of this great land, we're ready to reclaim our free-enterprising domination of it. Just follow the nifty examples and easy instructions in the next chapter.

CHAPTER TEN

THIS LAND WAS MADE FOR YOU AND BP

DURING THE 2008 REPUBLICAN National Convention, the liberal media seemed flummoxed by resounding cries of "Drill, baby, drill" led from the podium by industry shills and shrieked by all fifty delegations of pod-people from the remake of *Invasion of the Body Snatchers*. The chanting was a little creepy, OK. But why the flummoxation?

God gave us this vast, abundant land so we could plunder it. When the first Anglos arrived on the North American continent, they looked around and said, "Yo, lookit all this cheddar, mang!" They proceeded to slice up that cheddary wealth among the crackers: white, male property owners.

Looking at the original Constitution, before all those liberal nervous Nellies added hand-wringing amendments to extend those rich, cheesy opportunities to everybody, we can see who the founding fathers were really looking out for: themselves. This is only natural. Self-interest, baby, self-interest. Imagine how minorities or women might have written our Constitution. Yecch! Fortunately, Jesus and his disciples wrote the founding documents to benefit their own kind: well-to-do, white, educated, male land barons. They actually had the scratch and the know-how to get the economic engine of the New World going, and then give it some gas, let go of the steering wheel, and sit back as the vehicle of American enterprise ran down anything in its path.

Replacing the Church of England and the craft guilds of Europe with evangelical bootstrap capitalism, America's priesthood of fat-cat pillagers blessed this continent with the holy water of their sweat and shoved the communion wafers of their success in our faces. They laid the foundation of the country with their own bare hands (well, technically, with the bare hands of slaves, immigrants, and child laborers). By the late nineteenth century, these heroic industrialists had that foundation built, with most of the subflooring put in and the plumbing stubbed out, despite government's metaphorical building codes—or, better yet, with government's bribe-induced approval.

MEN ARE FROM MARS, BUSINESSMEN ARE FROM PLUTO

Industrialists quickly learned to share the wealth—not with workers or the poor (are you kidding?), but with lawmakers. This greased the wheels of industry and brought good old-fashioned self-interest to governing. Where's the incentive to work some boring government job if you can't earn serious, off-the-books payola? Free market capitalism creates a beautiful bond between private profiteer and public official. The result, according to editorial cartoonist Thomas Nast, is the plutocrat:

THE "BRAINS"

The Tea Party's worship of capitalism makes the plutocrat a stand-in for God. We love that guy! Not everyone, though, sees beauty in the classic caricature of Boss Tweed, commissioner of public works for New York City in the late 1800s. Most people find that faceless blob of moneygrubbing blubber kind of grotesque. And some have even likened it to the bland visage and bloated corpus of a more recent public official.

Now *there's* a commissioner of public works. More than any other alleged conservative, Dick "Dick" Cheney has blurred the line between private industrialist and government puppetmaster. Unlike dirty socialists, who try to blur that line by regulating the private sector, Cheney's genius was in privatizing the public sector. His plutocratic vision was of a for-profit government

Dick Cheney with collapsing American eagle.

whose partnership with business was essentially a series of joint ventures, mergers, and takeovers. Some of these start-ups produced war as their core product, with support services such as mayhem, falsifying intelligence, and outing American CIA agents. This ruthless bloodthirst is pretty impressive for a guy who got five deferments from the Vietnam draft because, as he said, "I had other priorities." But as he made clear throughout his vice-presidency, his real interest wasn't really in fighting *people*. Cheney has always had a bigger enemy: the natural environment. His instinct to profit from dominating and vanquishing nature drove him to become CEO of one of the world's greatest despoilers of land, water, and air: Halliburton.

A true multitasker, Cheney didn't even stop running the multinational energy conglomerate when he "retired" to "serve" at the "pleasure" of "President" George W. Bush. Instead, he remained on payroll, kept a half a million shares of stock, and showed up at board meetings when a wayward executive needed to be shot in the face. While moonlighting as vice president, Cheney stealthily achieved a takeover of the federal government by Halliburton and other private contractors.

EVERY PLUTOCRACY NEEDS A CEO

Cheney's first task in office, after eating several babies and drowning a bag of kittens in the Potomac, was to craft a new energy policy. After eight years of Clintonian communism and tree-hugging, we needed it! The Cheney energy task force turned oil, gas, coal, and nuclear industry executives into policymakers. Four years after their proposal, the Energy Policy Act of 2005 followed task force recommendations to the letter, if you make that letter a dollar sign. It was awesome.

The cornerstones of the new law exempted oil and gas exploration from the Safe Drinking Water Act of 1974/1986, leaving it to the states to decide how far up the ass to take Halliburton's drilling. The states bent over and obliged. This made it possible for energy companies to enrich groundwater with fabulous chemicals and fill the atmosphere with zesty gases at an unprecedented pace.

In the four years between the proposal and the passage of the law, Cheney cut funding for renewable energy and transformed the Minerals Management Service, which oversees oil and gas drilling, from a government watchdog to an industry bedfellow (literally—MMS employees accepted sexual favors and other gifts from dozens of lobbyists). And guess who was behind the drilling handiwork of the Deepwater Horizon well in the Gulf of Mexico? Yep, Halliburton. In collaboration with BP, Cheney and friends pulled off the biggest alteration of the natural environment since Michael Jackson's face.

That's how plutocrats deliver results to the nation even after leaving office—and with Cheney, they keep on pouring in! Free oil, right at our feet, on America's shores:

Chemicals injected into groundwater by hydraulic fracturing, free for the taking:

Chemical Constituent
1,2 Benzisothiazolin-2-one / 1,2-benzisothiazolin-3-one
1,2,4 trimethylbenzene
1,4-Dioxane

Chemical Constituent

1-eicosene

1-hexadecene

1-octadecene

1-tetradecene

2,2 Dibromo-3-nitrilopropionamide , a biocide

2,2′-azobis-{2-(imidazolin-2-yl)propane}-dihydrochloride

2,2-Dobromomalonamide

2-Acrylamido-2-methylpropane sulfonic acid sodium salt polymer

2-acryloyloxy ethyl (benzyl)dimethylammonium chloride

2-Bromo-2-nitro-1,3-propanediol

2-Butoxyethanol

2-Dibromo-3-Nitriloprionamide (2-Monobromo-3-nitriilopropionamide)

2-Ethylhexanol

2-Propanol / Isopropyl Alcohol / Isopropanol / Propan-2-ol

2-Propen-1-aminium, N,N-dimethyl-N-2-propenyl-chloride, homopolymer

2-propenoic acid, homopolymer, ammonium salt

2-Propenoic acid, polymer with 2 p-propenamide / Copolymer of acrylamide and sodium acrylate

2-Propenoic acid, polymer with sodium phosphinate (1:1)

2-propenoic acid, telomer with sodium hydrogen sulfite

Chemical Constituent
2-Propyn-1-ol / Propargyl alcohol
3,5,7-Triaza-1-azoniatricyclo[3.3.1.13,7]decane, 1-(3-chloro-2-propenyl)-chloride
3-methyl-1-butyn-3-ol
4-Nonylphenol Polyethylene Glycol Ether Branched / Nonylphenol ethoxylated / Oxyalkylated Phenol
Benzene, dodecylbenzene, naphthalene, kerosene, toluene, xylene, blowyatosmithereens
Acetic acid, hydroxy-, reaction products with triethanolamine
Acetic Anhydride
Acetone
Acrylamide and yippee, good old-fashioned formaldehyde

That's but a fraction of the fracking list, long kept a secret by the industry, in the same way that your mom protects old family recipes for natural gas chili or coal-slurry pie. But wait, there's more! In addition to offering this chemical bounty, hydraulic fracturing has also put straight-up natural gas into aquifers and water wells, giving many consumers free fuel mixed right into their drinking water! Hundreds of Americans can now light their tapwater on fire—and it's *natural*!

This scene is from *Gasland*, a documentary film by trouble-making banjo-player Josh Fox (on left in photo), who traveled the country intending to expose the damage done by the gas-drilling industry and ended up documenting its stunning generosity in providing this wealth of chemicals and fossil fuels—free—to any American citizen whose water supply is near a drilling site. It's as if Dick Cheney and his cronies were personally going door to door, handing out energy drinks. If the states will just let the frack-for-all continue while Obama's new EPA study plods ahead (results due in 2012), we could all be so lucky.

We can't let environmentalists poop this party with their anti-Dick regulations and insistence on so-called "clean water." Why should a few elite homeowners be the only ones to enjoy these free, gassy handouts?

Cheney's legacy doesn't stop there. It just keeps on giving. Look, more free oil, delivered by fish and waterfowl:

The bird here looks to be a common goose, with a few other oil-bearing critters nearby. But even visionary Dick Cheney may not have foreseen that the Gulf region's American wood stork, the endangered species responsible for delivering the nation's babies, also could be oil-lubricated, making baby delivery that much faster and easier.

As vice president, Cheney ensured that Halliburton's own subsidiary, KBR, won every defense contract it wanted in Iraq without even having to bid for them. Cheney also bribed every Nigerian official necessary to win multi-billion dollar energy contracts there. (Halliburton recently settled the bribery case out of court and went on its merry way about the globe. Without pesky environmental regulations in many developing countries, where Halliburton does half its business, it boggles the mind to imagine the world's resources served up à la Dick.) Cheney pulled all this off in a few short years, despite having a heart attack every other week or so. When does the guy sleep? What deep reserves of spiritual fuel fire the engines of his mastery in both public and private realms?

And what does this have to do with the Tea Party?

First things first. Dick Cheney returns each dawn, like Dracula, to a box of his native soil at an undisclosed location and sleeps for a few brief hours before applying a sun-protective coating of pancake TV makeup and beginning his day. His mastery of the military-industrial complex, the industrial-shitstorm complex, and the government-neglect-of-the-environment complex, is a function of the very heart that has proven so fragile and prone to infarction. Medical scans show Cheney's ticker to be not a typical human heart at all, but something far more rare: a hard-packed dirt clod attached to a pair of jumper cables. It's this remarkable organ that puts self-interest and profit before public service or, like, being human. He is the very model of a really Real American.

FREEDOM FROM THOUGHT

The implications for the Tea Party are clear. When we say we're for freedom and against government regulation, it's important not to think or feel. Thinking and feeling raise questions. You don't want to wonder if one American's freedom (Dick Cheney's, say) to deregulate natural gas drilling, sooner or later, is going to run into another American's freedom (yours, for example) to drink a glass of water without benzene in it. We can't have those kinds of doubts when we're yelling about liberal tree-huggers or enviro-nazis putting regulatory straitjackets on industry. We need the kind of surly, unreflective self-confidence that Dick Cheney displays every time he says something that turns out to be completely false.

When you're loudly denying global warming, or protesting your taxes being used to support Obama's EPA study of hydraulic fracturing, just remember how Dick Cheney assured us, for instance, that the Iraq insurgency was "in its last throes." Amazing, how he said it with such quiet authority while, even as he spoke, insurgents were gathering momentum to reach new heights of violence over the next two years. If you're arguing with a liberal who's going on and on about melting ice and rising sea levels, just say (with quiet authority), "Greenland's ice sheet is actually thickening, not thinning." This turns out to be true in the middle of Greenland, where increased precipitation from warmer temperatures is adding to the ice sheet. It's just not true around the vast edges, where Greenland is losing 200 km^3 of ice annually, double the rate from a decade ago. (Cubic kilometers are alarmingly big. In order to put a few of those ice cubes in a drink, you'd have to have a glass the size of Mt. Kilauea, the second-biggest active volcano in Hawaii.) *Don't think about that.* All you'll do is raise doubts. There is no room for doubt in the Tea Party. Leave that crap to the wafflers, the intellectuals. The liberals.

SMOKING CRATERS OF SELECTIVE TRUTH

Speaking of volcanoes, this book is about to blow up some other global warming arguments. That's the big issue, after all, with socialists trying to cramp our capitalist style and sequester our carbon and set American industry back a thousand years to when people used the sun for heat and stuff like that. Conservatives can win this battle without conserving anything except our right to do whatever the hell we want. Lucky for us, environmental science is so huge and multi-faceted that you can always find a few scientific outliers—and sometimes, just liars—with convincing arguments that support a pro-business, anti-thought agenda. Remember, you've got millions of dollars behind you in industry-funded research, providing selectively "true" evidence to support almost any claim you want to make. Here are a few of the usual liberal arguments to score some Real American points against, and some pesky science not to think about:

Sheryl Crow, admittedly somewhat hot.

1. The "unprecedented" argument: Singer-activist-annoyer Sheryl Crow's **liberal point:** "The planet has been heating up for the last century and is now reaching unprecedented levels, man. A change would do you good."

Real American "true" counterpoint: "That's 'My Favorite Mistake,' Sheryl. It was hotter than this six thousand years ago in the Holocene Climatic Optimum."

(Ed. Note: The Holocene was hotter only in the northern hemisphere during the summer. Globally, based on all the data we have, the hottest period in history is the last one hundred years. But don't think about that, Boyle, or your little brain will burst into flame.)

Al Gore receives the Nobel Hockey Prize.

2. The "hockey stick" argument: Insane Democrat loser Al Gore's **liberal point:** "The so-called hockey stick graph shows temperatures averaged over millennia as a fairly straight line, with an anomalous spike moving sharply upward from the twentieth century on."

Real American "true" counterpoint: "The hockey stick is broken. While you were sexually harassing a masseuse, Al, that graph, the foundation of global warming theory, was proven invalid."

(Ed. Note: The hockey stick graph isn't the foundation of any theory. It's one of many studies that show dramatically rising global temperatures—and it wasn't proven invalid. After corrections to this study's methodology, the result remains: like every

temperature reconstruction we have, it shows the twentieth century to be the warmest ever, with the most dramatic rise after 1920. Slapshot! Don't look now, Boyle, but science just put another one in the back of the net.)

3. The "rising sea levels" argument: Actor-activist-playboy Leonardo DiCaprio's **liberal point:** "Due to melting ice, sea levels are rising. A small rise of 400 mm. could cover 11 percent of Bangladesh's coast, creating ten million climate refugees."

Real American "true" counterpoint: "Arctic sea levels are actually falling, which you'd know if you weren't as retarded as your character in *What's Eating Gilbert Grape?*"!

(Ed Note: How about some actual science, Boyle? Sea levels rise and fall unevenly around the globe, due to several causes. True, recent satellite data (from a study not yet peer-reviewed), shows local sea levels in the Arctic falling slightly over the last ten years. Even if the study turns out to be correct, it doesn't mean global sea levels are falling, because they're not. Seas worldwide have been rising ±1.8 mm. per year for the past century. Some scientists' pants are already wet over it.)

Leo lookin' like a slicked-up shifty liberal.

4. The "ten hottest years" argument: NASA scientist-activist James Hansen's **liberal point:** "The ten hottest years on Earth all took place since 1997."

Real American "true" counterpoint: "Ha! Temperatures trend *down* after 1998! Global warm-

James Hansen testifies between arrests.

ing ended, except for your overheated fear-mongering!"

(Ed. Note: Better start singing "la la la" with your fingers in your ears, Boyle: Yes, 1998 was a hot one, topping previous record-holder 1997 by .2 degrees C. But 1998 spiked above the over-all warming trend due to the strongest El Niño of the century. To "prove" a cooling trend followed 1998 by cherry-picking that year (and ignoring James Hansen's NASA numbers, which show 2005 to be even hotter) is like isolating a year of explosive population growth, pointing to a few slightly less-explosive years that follow, and saying, "Lookie, population is decreasing." By every measure we have, average global temperatures are rising. Good thing your denial can rise even higher!)

5. The "global warming is manmade" argument: Lastly, some random dirty socialist makes this **liberal point:** "Overwhelming scientific evidence points to human activity producing the high concentrations of CO_2 that contribute to

Trotsky tries to look like Leonardo DiCaprio.

global warming, comrade." Last-ditch onslaught of **Real American "true" counterpoints:** "More CO_2 occurs naturally than from human activity. CO_2 fluctuations have always occurred anyway—and temperatures rise *before* CO_2 does, so there's no causal effect, you dirty commie. So there."

(Ed. Note: *Try to keep up, Boyle. Yes, CO_2 does fluctuate naturally, but in 150 years, CO_2 from human activity has equaled increases that used to take five to ten thousand years to accumulate. Unlike nature, which cyclically pulls carbon back out of the atmosphere, we're only adding to it, so atmospheric concentrations that were relatively stable throughout history have now risen by 35 percent. And yes, CO_2 lags behind temperature, but climatic feedback means that the ultimate magnitude of temperature change is largely determined by CO_2 levels, now at all-time highs—and that doesn't even include blowhard arguments or human breathing, which science invites all global warming deniers to stop.)*

Speaking of arguments, we need the best rhetoric money can buy. The liberal edge in writers means the left can create compelling, heart-stirring political rhetoric. Put an argument like that in a good actor's mouth, directed by Steven Spielberg or any of the hoards of liberal directors out there, and it's trouble. But we've got a few writers and directors of our own. Perhaps most importantly, one of our big-name writers had a philosophy that influenced American politics more than any dirty commie Trotsky Chomsky the left can claim. We've got Ayn Rand.

This book searched in vain for a free, public domain image of Ayn Rand. The whole concept of public domain is anti-Ayn; you can't get her for free. Even her government-issued (and thus, ironic) postage stamp costs thirty-three cents, and collectors have now driven up that price to a full half-dollar. And it's not even a good likeness (she was a snaggle-toothed hag). But the stamp's designer, Nick Gaetano, has captured something essential about this heroic, Russian-American champion of industry, as she peers out at us from behind a façade of soulless architecture, while standing in a capitalist golden shower. Rand's a vision of a world plundered for profit is like pornography for plutocrats, and has guided anti-environmental policy for decades.

FROM RUSSIA, WITH LOVE OF MONEY

The hero of Ayn Rand's *The Fountainhead* is architect Howard Roark, a manly man who's so completely self-contained that the world outside his own ego might as well not exist—except that he needs it for building sites and materials and what-not. The what-not includes his womanly woman, who falls for him when he rapes her. It's the kind of book where the hero says stuff like, "I never think of myself in relation to anyone else," and Rand means for us to admire him for it. She wants to inspire us with the vision of guys who say, "When I see mountain peaks, I think of tunnels and dynamite."

Then there's *Atlas Shrugged*, the ultimate expression of Ayn Rand's gift for stupefying dullness. More sermon than novel, its sanctimonious heroes (John Galt, above all) spout Rand's philosophy to pathetic loser villains (us), like so: "Until and unless you discover that money is the root of all good, you ask for your own destruction...Blood, whips and guns—or dollars. Take your choice—there is no other." If you slog through the zillion pages of this tedium, though, you'll realize that you can have it both ways. Pay money (good) to buy the book, and then, by the time its lacerating prose (evil) has whipped you into submission, you'll beg someone to blow your brains out.

Real Americans love to invoke Ayn Rand. The "Who Is John Galt?" and "I Am John Galt" and "Atlas Is Gettin' Shruggy Widdit" signs showed up at the first Tax Day rallies in 2009. Libertarians are the biggest Rand fans (Ron Paul named his son for her), carrying that banner of self-interest in their push for lower taxes, free markets, and rule by big capital rather than big government. They don't care if Ayn Rand was an atheist. They don't even seem to mind that, in the last years of her life, after years of bitching about social services and those who benefit from them, she was drawing Social Security, or that she made heavy use of Medicare in her losing battle with lung cancer. We can't expect integrity from anyone born in Russia, and her embrace of contradiction should be a model for all of us who can talk the talk all day long but would rather ride an Amigo than walk the walk. Some conservatives do deplore Rand's atheism. They'd prefer

Howard Roark and John Galt to be God-fearing assholes instead of self-worshiping assholes. But one thing we can all agree on, as Rand's heroes bossily confirm: nature is our bitch. It's here to be assaulted, raped, exploited for profit. We'll buy tickets to that.

So why didn't we buy tickets to the movie version of *Atlas Shrugged (Part One)*, which came out on Tax Day, 2011? This $20 million dollar propaganda film made less than $5 million at the box office. Those who did see it tend to use the phrase "train wreck" to describe it, which sounds exciting. Guess not!

Assuming investors are willing to lose more money, we'll be treated to *Part Two: Still Shruggin'* and *Part Three: The Browbeating*, featuring John Galt's heroic speech (in the book, it's several jillion pages of sanctimonious scolding). Sounds like great cinema, doesn't it? Hours of some egomaniac's verbal wanking? It's gotta be better than slogging through the book. In fact, if you haven't read *Atlas Shrugged*, just watch the trailer on YouTube. It'll save you hundreds of grueling hours of having the same point drilled into your skull over and over.

Drill, baby, drill. Isn't that where this chapter started? Isn't that how Dick Cheney, the Howard Roark of government architects, the John Galt of plutocratic engineers, pursued his American dream with no thought of his relation to anyone else, with the almighty dollar his ultimate value, hundreds of millions in his pocket from the plunder of a world he couldn't care less about? Is there a better expression of Real America than those three words, one of them repeated so the chant isn't too challenging for unthinking people to memorize?

Drill. The perfect technological metaphor for rape. *Baby.* A great word for the intellectual level of the chanting masses themselves, little lambs bleating their way to the end of days, baa-baa-ing all the way to bye-bye. And *drill* again. Keep on drilling, baby, until we emerge in China just as we imagined we could as children. China, where they invest twice what the United States does in alternative energy every year. China, the world's largest producer of solar photovoltaics. China, where American experts project that all electricity will be solar-, hydro-, wind-, geothermal-, and biomass-generated by the year 2030. But for now, thank God, China burns more coal than anybody on earth. They may be dirty commies, but at least they're not full-blown tree-huggers. Their air is unbreathable and they're poisoning their water by hydraulic fracturing like there's no tomorrow, so all that expert crap about 2030 is moot. They'll be just as dead as we will. Then we'll see who God likes best.

This book thinks we already know the answer to that. The Chinese will go to hell and Real Americans will be streaming through the pearly gates like oil-lubricated storks, baby. Why? Because for all our self-interest and greed and fiddling while our home planet burns, Real Americans have always put God right up there with Country. We believe the two are inseparable. The next and final chapter is really just one big fat prayer that it may always be so in America, by God.

CHAPTER ELEVEN

★★★

WHY JESUS WROTE THE CONSTITUTION

REVOLUTION REQUIRES BREAKING THE law. Jesus did it. So did the rest of the original Tea Party. We Teabaggers certainly talk a good game, waving guns around as we talk, but how do we know when the righteousness of our cause transcends our duty as citizens to abide by stupid ol' laws and the Constitution we claim to revere?

Remember back to Chapter 8, Principle #5? To paraphrase: good laws are divinely inspired, and bad laws are the devil's handiwork. How do you know if a law is good or bad? Look it up in the Bible. We have laws against murder, based on the Ten Commandments' proscription against killing and also on our own moral sense that murder is a bummer. We have laws against rape, despite Ayn Rand glorifying it in her books. And of course, many freedoms were guaranteed to us by our Creator and the framers of the Constitution, who did their best to prevent bad laws, if you don't count the Three-Fifths Compromise. This book doesn't count it, because, ick, fractions.

So, has bad law actually made its way into the Constitution? Of course it has! Liberal legislators and activist judges routinely infect our precious founding document with socialism. In 1913, the Sixteenth Amendment authorized the income tax, causing George Washington to roll over so violently in his grave that he kicked right into the next grave over and crushed Martha's skull.

There was also a close call on the Equal Rights Amendment of 1972. Remember when that destroyed the American family and turned every public restroom into a sex dungeon and forced women to have abortions while being drafted—just like Phyllis Schlafly said it would—so some states decided not to ratify it and others changed their minds and rescinded it, so it expired ten years later? Whew. Aren't white men in enough trouble in this country, hounded on all sides by minority rights? And feminazis want equal rights for other genders, too? Where does it all end, Lord?

Speaking of Him, let's not forget that awful year of our Lord, 1919, when prohibitionists threw a gigantic wet blanket over the entire length of the Republic and pooped both parties into passing the Eighteenth Amendment, God help us. And then, God did help us! He gave His only begotten Son back to us for a few days in 1933[1] to turn water into

1 In June 1933, the Rev. William Branham was baptizing sinners in the Ohio River when a Pillar of Fire descended and a voice said unto him, "You are sent forth something something the second coming of Christ something." The roaring fire made it hard to hear, but the sinners said it was awesome. Anyway, no one ever reported a Jesus sighting, but Prohibition got repealed and later Ronald

wine, repealing Prohibition and letting America drink the sweet alcohol of freedom again, after a long, dry spell of fourteen years. Thank you, Jesus! Why that miracle is so often overlooked by historians and teachers, this book does not understand. Or does it?!

OUR GODLESS LIBERAL SCHOOLS

Before we discuss all the ways in which the Progressive agenda has ruined the republic, corrupted our children, and taken the Christ out of Christmas, let's all put our right hands over our hearts and recite the Pledge of Allegiance:

> I pledge allegiance to the flag
> of the United States of America,
> and to the republic for which it stands,
> one nation **UNDER GOD**, indivisible,
> with liberty and justice for all. Amen.

Liberal historians like to point out that the pledge was actually written for schoolchildren by a socialist, Francis Bellamy, which explains why the original version, published in a children's magazine in 1892, did NOT include the phrase "under God." They'll also tell you that that the Pledge has been altered four times, and that it was only the last time,

---

Reagan became president. So saying Jesus came back in 1933 is no crazier than any other historical claims made by the Tea Party.

in 1954, that God made it into the final draft. Look at these kids, back in 1899:

They don't even know how to put their hands over their hearts right! They're doing karate chops against their chests, probably because that socialist Francis Bellamy studied kung fu in Red China. If you multiply this scene across the nation, with every child in every public school reciting that godless pledge for sixty-two years, is it any wonder that the Christian foundation of this country has crumbled into a pile of liberal gravel? But wait, it gets worse:

That's the famed "Bellamy salute." This book is not kidding. You can't make this stuff up. It turns out that the author of the Pledge of Allegiance was a total fascist. In 1942, with half the Western world doing Nazi salutes to Der Führer, even a president as liberal as FDR could see the creepiness of American kids starting their day with a collective "flag heil." So Roosevelt stopped shtupping his secretary long enough to institute the palm-over-the-heart salute as part of the Flag Code. Also, because Roosevelt was a commie, "under God" was still out, and the Flag Code didn't get put into the Constitution.

It took a Christian minister working together with a Republican president to finally get God into the Pledge. George M. Docherty and Dwight D. Eisenhower met at church and quickly became lovers. Like Mamie, Docherty called Eisenhower "God" in bed, because Ike required it. And Ike was definitely a "top"—thus, the private joke between the two men, with a punch line involving the phrase "under

God." Although the affair had ended by the time a bill to add those words to the Pledge came before the president, he signed it with a wistful smile, and later said, "Every time I say the pledge, I think of George." Most people think he meant Washington, but this book has strayed dreamily from the point. The point is that everything was good in America at first, then went bad because of godlessness, communism, and fascism (which is redundant—it's all the same Progressive agenda), then got good again in 1954 for a few brief, shining years, and then went bad again. Just look at a typical elementary school schedule from the early 1900s:

- ➡ 5:30–7:00: Walk five miles uphill in the snow to get indoctrinated at school
- ➡ 7:00–7:15: Roll call, announcements, godless Pledge of Allegiance with fascist salute
- ➡ 7:15–7:30: Schnapps & vodka shots
- ➡ 7:30–8:30: Split into two reading groups: *Das Kapital* vs. *Mein Kampf*
- ➡ 8:30–9:30: Class struggle
- ➡ 9:30–10:30: Recess
- ➡ 10:30–11:00: Math and science (labor theory of value and dialectic materialism)
- ➡ 11:00–12:00: Lunch[2]
- ➡ 12:00–1:00: Marching, shouting in unison, firebombing, fleeing from authorities

---

2 A typical school lunch menu: Pigs in Bunkers, Dictator-tots with "Blood of the Workers" ketchup, and Proletariat Pie.

- 1:00–2:00: Recess
- 2:00–3:00: Beer Hall Putsch
- 3:00: Moral collapse, school dismissed

Parents and educators who wonder why American math and science teaching has been so weak need look no further than a day in the life of a child during that tragic period in American history (and you'll notice there's no American history on the schedule). Compare that values-destroying school day with this, from the late 1950s:

- 6:45–7:00: Skip along tidy suburban streets to neighborhood school
- 7:00–8:00: Invocation, flag ceremony, hand-over-heart "under God" Pledge/loyalty oath
- 8:00–8:30: Doughnuts and sharing the Good News around the milk cooler
- 8:30–9:30: Reading (*Dick & Jane*, *Silas Marner*) and 'Riting (sermons, stern essays)
- 9:30–10:30: 'Rithmetic, brought to you by GM and Standard Oil
- 10:30–11:30: Science, brought to you by the Southern Baptist Convention
- 11:30–12:00: Blessing and lunch[3]

---

3 A typical menu: All-Right Hamburger®, Hegemony Grits™, Sunshine Salad^WTF? (*Jello with carrots*), and Orange Drink (*enriched water with orange crayon swirled around in it*).

⇒ 12:00–1:00: Recess
⇒ 1:00–1:30: Art/music (drawing inside the lines, group singing of "Marching to Pretoria")
⇒ 1:30–2:30: Civics/American history, brought to you by The John Birch Society
⇒ 2:30–3:00: Ethnocentric, middle-class standardized test
⇒ 3:00: Benediction, dismissal, home to serve parents, God, and country

It was a glorious moment in American education, that small, stained-glass window of time between 1954 and the mid-1960s. Aided by wholesome, righteous television programming and patriotic, alcoholic zealots like Senator Joe McCarthy, we routed filthy communism from our public institutions. America was all good again. When Eisenhower left office he gave the Democrats a booming economy, Kennedy put a hot, charming First Lady on the throne in Camelot, and once we got past that pesky Cuban missile crisis, it seemed that we were invincible. We were on our way to the moon, the stars, and of course, church. Then to the shopping mall, as provided for in the Bill of Rights.

But the Progressive agenda is like dog poop on America's shoe. We think we've got it all scraped off, but suddenly there's a whiff of crappy communist conspiracy, and a president gets shot in a motorcade as it passes by a book depository, a grassy knoll, and a bunch of Cuban nationals on the Soviet payroll with links to the CIA, the Mafia, the Freemasons, and don't even start about the Council on

Foreign Relations. While this book applauds the marksmanship and the general idea of removing Democrats from office, it must be admitted that the Kennedy assassination was a great blow to America's bright, mid-century prospects. Those who got the terrible news in Miss McPherson's second-grade class at Luff Elementary School, and didn't want to intrude upon their grieving teacher to ask to use the restroom, may be excused if they ended up wetting their pants, which no one would have known about if Lance Graham hadn't laughed and pointed it out. Oh, it was a tragic day all around.

The tragedy reverberated down the long, bleak corridor of the following decades. Kennedy's death was part of God's plan, of course, but it ironically caused many of us to doubt God's goodness. We even doubted America's supremacy. What was the point of pledging our allegiance to a country if its handsomest, Marilyn Monroe-boffingest president could be cut down in his prime? Liberalism once again reared its Putinesque head, got the nation's kids all hopped-up on false drugs, and installed lazy hippies and socialist perverts on school faculties to teach folk singing, world cultures, and sex education. In less time than it takes to make a macramé bong-holder, America's public schools went from being the greatest in the world to not-even-close-to-being-the-greatest in the world. By the end of the twentieth century, the United States ranked so low on standardized test scores compared with other developed nations that an American ambassador was dispatched to make excuses to the international community, but couldn't read the street address of the U.N. building because he was mathematically illiterate.

Is it any wonder? Look at this typical Midwestern school day from 1974, when the '60s finally arrived from the coast, invading the rest of the country:

➡ 7:30–8:00-ish: Get high in VW microbus en route to school

➡ 8:00–ish: Straggle into class, parody version of Pledge with faux-military salute

➡ 8:30, maybe: Interpretive dance and mime

➡ 9–something: Poetry: the lyrics of Bob Dylan, Joan Baez, and James Brown[4]

➡ 10 or, like, 11: Free time/drug-dealing/string art

➡ Mid-day: Munchies[5]

➡ 1:00 or so: Phys ed (Frisbee, hackysack) and Advanced Atheism

➡ Around 2:00: American history according to the ACLU and Noam Chomsky

➡ 3–whatever: Student demonstration with sing-along (clocks smashed, school bell destroyed, fire alarms set off, arrests, school shutdown)

---

4 *James Brown lyrics were often used to accompany sex education classes as well.*

5 *Salisbury Seitan, Raw Veggie Succotash, Charred Flag Chips, Tofu-Carob Brownies, and Hemp Milk.*

This decline took place in a single decade of rampant liberalism. Within another decade, students were in charge. And Clinton's '90s culminated in school shootings with students unable to defend themselves because guns were outlawed, ensuring that only outlaws had guns. Why? It's easy to blame the NEA, lax academic standards, parental permissiveness, video games, Hollywood, or a general decline in morality at large.

These are all contributing factors. But the real question is, why the moral decline, and what can we do about it? (Also, why did they have to put carrots in Jello, the one failing of our schools during the late 1950s and early 1960s? But we can wait for an answer to that while addressing the other question about moral decline or whatever.)

UP AGAINST THE NON-EXISTENT WALL

The answer, as usual, is simple. The decline of our schools parallels our decline as a God-fearing, Paul Revere-ing, profiteering Christian nation. We have forgotten the Christ-y crust and the delicious toppings of our heritage, and instead liberal historians have substituted the devil's tofu: secular humanism. We the People, the Tea Party, are recovering from years of liberal indoctrination, striving to reweave the torn and tangled moral fibers of our youth into a tapestry, or at least an area rug, of Christianity and consumerism. These are the two legs upon which the Real American body politic stands. But now it must kneel. Because, to sum it up, all our problems can be solved by a single act: school prayer.

It's a bigger act than that, really, because in order to get prayer in schools, we have to break down the "wall" between church and state in this country. We're getting there. State boards of education in Texas and Kansas have struck mighty blows against that wall, crusading for religious content in public school curricula. These school board members aren't just Monday-morning throwbacks; they live their straight-and-narrow faith every day.

In fact, when the Texas School Board convened on May 18, 2010, to review social studies curricula, they kicked it olde school with a prayer by Cynthia Dunbar, who got her college degree from Pat Robertson's "University." At least, it started out as a prayer. It did veer into more of a statement of political belief as Ms. Dunbar described America as "a Christian land, governed by Christian principles." Let's listen in:

> I believe that no one can read the history of our country without realizing that the Good Book and the Spirit of the Savior have, from the beginning, been our guiding geniuses…I believe the entire Bill of Rights came into being because of the knowledge our forefathers had of the Bible, and their belief in it…I like to believe we are living today in the spirit of the Christian religion. I like also to believe that as long as we do, no great harm can come to our country. All this I pray, in the name of my Lord and Savior, Jesus Christ. Amen.

Jesus Christ, indeed. Now *that* is a school prayer, people. It's that kind of testifyin' that gives educators the strength to rewrite history textbooks, as the Texas School Board does. Texas, see, buys kerjillions of schoolbooks, so they're influential with publishers, who don't tend to put out individual state versions of their books. As goes Texas, so goes the nation.

And here's how Texas goes: in 2010, they replaced the words "slave trade" with the "Atlantic triangular trade." All former references to "capitalism" now read "free enterprise" (after all, there are no slaves in this history, just triangles, floating free on the Atlantic). Best of all, their list of great thinkers who influenced the American Revolution no longer features pesky Thomas "wall of separation" Jefferson (who famously took scissors to his Bible and reassembled it without all the miracles). It's got St. Thomas Aquinas now. And instead of having to study boring old John Locke as an intellectual whose ideas on law the founders admired, Texas

Israelites carry an ark full of covenant and new textbooks into Jericho.

kids can now study Moses and Biblical law. In history class. Amen.

And of course, there's Kansas, with its famous school board decision to remove the teaching of evolution from the science curriculum. That has since been modified, because even in Kansas, liberals sometimes get on school boards and thwart God's plan. So rather than a rewritten curriculum, Kansas kids get a watered-down version of doubts about Darwin's wacky theory, which may come up on state assessment tests.

The battle rages on. Bringing down that wall will take faith and persistence, as it did for the Israelites who went up against Jericho's public school system (Joshua 6:1).

BUT. If you think we can just march around in a circle seven times and blow a big blast on a ram's horn to knock down that wall, well, good luck. Because this is the ultimate battleground between Real America and Fake (liberal) America, and the Progressive agenda is not just going to sit there rolling doobies and let you win the battle. It's going to suit up, grab every weapon of logic and legal precedent and Lucifer available, and sooner or later, it's going to hire a fancy lawyer like Laurence Tribe or Seth Waxman to represent it before the Supreme Court. These guys are like really well-read, vicious wolverines of liberalism, going for the throat of institutions on behalf of civil liberties and Satan. They will gargle the blood of the Tea Party and stuff our severed testicles into Ruth Bader Ginsburg's purse. It's going to be a wall-out battle. It will require all the resources we have.

BALLS, NOT WALLS

You'd think it would be easy, because our founding documents don't spell out the need for the separation of church and state at all. As El Supremo, Antonin Scalia, might say, "Go ahead, show me the wall. Show me the separation." If a liberal's stupid enough to take the bait and quote the First Amendment, "Congress shall pass no law respecting the establishment of religion," Scalia will tear 'em a new one, insisting that the Establishment Clause was never intended to limit the religious life of Americans, but to prevent government from giving one religion preferential treatment over others. (Sometimes El Supremo's doctrine of "originalism" has to wander pretty far from the original source in order to make a Scaliargument®.) If the hapless liberal quotes the famous letter by Thomas Jefferson that uses the phrase "wall of separation between church and state," or the Treaty of Tripoli in which John Adams specifically says that "the Government of the United States of America was not, in any sense, founded on the Christian religion," Scalia will point out that letters and treaties by a couple of guys who showed up at the Constitutional Convention of 1787 are NOT the Constitution. And he may conclude by snarling, "Bafangu, you liberal ass," and throwing

El Supremo, the dark lord of originalism.

his barbed-wire Opus Dei necklace like a ninja star in the face of his vanquished foe.

Scalia's ferocious, originalist approach to the Constitution is the same kind of selective literalism that Real Americans apply to the Bible. It makes him a big states-rights guy, as all Real Americans should be. But he's perfectly willing to abandon all that if the results suit his ideology, as we saw in *Gore v. Bush*, when Scalia ended the vote recount ordered by the Florida Supreme Court and installed Bush as president.

El Supremo is religious as all get-out. But he doesn't let the Great Whore of Catholicism boss him around. A Grand Wizard in Opus Dei, he doesn't even answer to a priest or bishop, but runs his own show within the religion, cozying up to popes or vice presidents whose cases are being heard by the Court, and whoever else he wants to hang with. Like his fellow Mafioso, Frank Sinatra, he's done it his way from an early age, skyrocketing through a brilliant academic career and into the law, leaving a wake of stunned liberals and nine children behind. With those brass balls, and his combative, question-peppering style at the bench, he's the guy we count on to demolish the arguments of fancy lawyers trying to trowel more mortar onto the wall between church and state that we're going to take down.

(To keep up with Scalia's work on behalf of theocracy, big business, and his prodigious drinking and sex habits, follow @Scalia_Bafangu on Twitter.)

WHO'S PLAYING FOR TEAM GOD?

But Scalia can't do it alone. Who else is on our side (other than God, Jesus, and a few scattered school boards)? Well, we've got the other three conservative justices:

"Coke-pube"
Thomas

"Oath-botch"
Roberts

"Scalia-bottom"
Alito

We may also have the swing justice, "Li'l Tony" Kennedy. His Tea may be lukewarm, but his swing votes in cases decided 5–4 go to the pious conservative wing twice as often as to the godless liberal wing. Interestingly, all four of these justices are Catholics, too, which means they may be getting secret instructions from Rome. Fortunately, the current pope is a super-duper conservative, so full-bore WASPs shouldn't worry too much about the Illuminati dictating jurisprudence to the Supremes.

We've also got plenty of piety in the legislative branch. The GOP leadership is all about the Jesus, and they're listening to the Tea Party more than they used to, since we flexed our muscles in the 2010 mid-terms. Some of our staunchest allies—Jim DeMint, Michele Bachmann, Rand Paul—may not be in official leadership positions, but they're bossy loudmouths and they're slowly wearing away mainstream Republican Party resistance to extreme ideological positions. Like Sarah Palin and Glenn Beck, they're willing to push back against the establishment AND the Establishment Clause. That wall is going to crumble, and when it does, church and state are going to rush into each other's arms like East and West Berlin after the fall of communism. What we need, as a moral people threatened by secularism, postmodernism, and other things we don't really understand, is for religion to tap that government ass.

The great thing is, we know how to do it, thanks to the gas and oil industry. As payback for funding the Bush/Cheney campaign and helping them get elected—well, installed—hundreds of oil and gas flunkies ended up as federal employees in the Interior Department (especially the MMS), the EPA, and the Justice Department. By the end of 2001, these gigantic sinkholes of government oversight were so full up with Texas oil men, you couldn't bend over in Washington without getting *Brokeback*ed by a pretend cowboy. These are people who helped Cheney deliver the free oil onto our beaches and put the free gas in our tap water, a great example for all nice Christians to follow. The rest of corporate America joined the oil and gas industries in making sweet love to government, as if to show the religious right the way.

CORPORATE MONEY LAUNDERERS HAVE FEELINGS, TOO

In the 2010 *Citizens United v. Federal Election Commission* decision, the Supreme Court affirmed that corporations were "persons," and thus could enjoy the First Amendment's freedom of speech protections. In a 5–4 majority opinion (thanks, Li'l Tony!), the Supreme Court ditched the word "speech" and instead gave corporations the freedom to "pour a ginormous crapload of corporate money into political campaigns." And they pulled this off just in time to open the floodgates on the midterm elections.

Candidates in 2010 offered themselves for purchase at premium prices, and corporate donors paid as never before—a 384 percent increase over the 2006 midterms in campaign spending by outside groups (seriously, a 384% increase! This book didn't even make that up!). For example, Karl Rove's "American Crossroads" group raised tens of millions of dollars from oil, real estate, health care, and agribusiness corporations, and reported spending some $38 million of it on targeted political races, offering money and advertising muscle to conservative campaigns faster than the candidates could say, "God bless America."

God did indeed shower America with a warm, golden stream of blessings through this landmark decision, writing the name "capitalism" in the snows of January 2010. And Obama's objection to the Court's ruling just proved him a godless heathen. Capitalism, after all, is the religion of corporations, with its "Invisible Hand" (the mystical higher power of the marketplace), doctrines of deregulation and *caveat emptor*, and rituals of stock-market fervor and board-of-trade speaking in tongues, all presided over by a priesthood of fat-cat bankers, brokers, financial whiz-kids, and government officials. Capitalism is the one religion in the world whose power surpasses that of the Vatican and the international Jewish banking conspiracy combined—because it contains them both. As its deacons (PACs, 527 organizations, and 501(c)(4) groups) passed offering plates down the corporate pews and its devotees filled them with cash, it became clear that the *Citizens United* case wasn't about freedom of speech. It was about freedom of religion.

That's good for the right. Conservative groups raised double the amount that liberal groups did, and got results.

Aside from the few Tea Party losses detailed in Chapter 2, power changed hands in a conservative landslide, giving the House back to the GOP, along with the car, the kids, and the dog, as the voting public divorced Democrats and their Progressive agenda in a bitter battle for the custody of America's future.

Best of all, the reporting rules on donations were gutted by the *Citizens United* ruling, so that only one dollar out of every four spent on 2010 campaigns got reported. The truth is, we don't know how much money was raised, how much was spent, or how much was pocketed and blown on gay hookers. This effectively rolled back campaign finance reform not just to the pre-McCain-Feingold days, but to the pre-Teddy Roosevelt days of banking trusts and graft-happy political bosses. As Ralph Nader was heard to say after reading the Supreme Court decision, "Holy shit, my career has been for nothing."

THE FUTURE OF THE GRAND OLD TEA PARTY

Corporate/religious investment in conservative candidates works. Karl Rove's group won nine of twelve Senate races in which it spent money, including (as far as we know— remember, reporting rules are looser than a bathhouse for Catholic priests) the campaigns of these two smokin' hot Tea Party candidates, now the youngest members of the U.S. Senate.

Mike Lee (R–UT)   *Marco Rubio (R–FL)*

Well, "smokin' hot" doesn't apply to Mike Lee, who's about as sexy as a square dance at a Mormon compound (one of his favorite activities) and who has a annoying penchant for self-righteous clichés and complete bullshit. OK, so the guy's a douche. At least he's *our* douche.

But watch out for Marco Rubio. The photo above is not even a good picture of this GQ-caliber young tyro, whose Cuban-quarterback-lookin' face is the future of American conservatism. And this book can see that future. This bold, clairvoyant book is going on record with a prediction, right here and now (April 29, 2011, two days from the publisher's deadline, so this may come from too much coffee and too little sleep): *Marco Rubio will be on the GOP national ticket in 2016 and will sweep into office, bringing Tea Party values to the White House for the first time since Ronald Reagan brought them in 1980.* (Reagan immediately lost them, then forgot that he'd brought them at all, except for a brief period during his reelection campaign.) It will be a patriotic kick in the pants to watch Rubio, only thirty-nine when he came to Washington, grow into a seasoned panderer over the next few years, navigating minefields of compromise and tap-dancing for the media when his ambitions run afoul of his values. He's already shown great have-it-both-ways instincts, regularly attending Catholic mass and a Protestant megachurch. A father of four and married to a former Miami Dolphins cheerleader, he's a likeable, telegenic, Tea Party dreamboat. The first thing Rubio did when he took office was to hire a former top Cheney advisor as his chief of staff. Does this choirboy know his way around the rectory of American politics, or what?!

Speaking of Cheney, conservatives may say, what's this presumption of Rubio bringing Tea Party values to the White House "for the first time" since Reagan? Aren't we forgetting a certain plutocratic patriot? Sorry, Cheney's Tea Party cred only extends to his ravaging of the environment for personal gain. The Dickster helped to expand the federal government rather than shrink it. He weakened national security (or maybe you don't care about sabotaging CIA agents' careers and endangering their operations and then letting a guy named Scooter take the fall for you). And Cheney's obsession with secrecy, back-door deals, and man-sized office safes made government creepier and less accountable to We the People. He also raised a lesbian daughter, which means he didn't apply the Growing-Up-Extremely-Right Principles (they hadn't really been formulated yet, but anyone with

Cheney's super powers should have been able to look into the future and see them). The guy actually supports gay marriage, which is not only a threat to the sanctity of marriage, but to the sanctity of this book, and also to the sanctity of the book of Leviticus, on which the Constitution is arguably based.[6]

VARIATIONS ON A THEOCRAPLUTOLIGAREPUBLIC

But Cheney did show us the way, giving us the industry model for how religion can climb into bed with government and make the beast with two backs. That's how we do it, Teabaggers. With a massive fund-raising effort in the 2012 election, leveraging the campaign financing freedoms brought to us by the Roberts Supreme Court, we can put the right people in office and then hold their left feet to the fire when it comes to appointing the right federal judges, mid-level bureaucrats, and low-level functionaries who will bend the arc of history toward just us Christians. By the time Marco Rubio takes office in 2016, the U.S. government won't be a plutocracy anymore. It'll be an oligarepublutotheocracy.

Now, lefties will decry this strategy, with their usual offensive accusation: that the religious right's insistence on America being a Christian nation is no better than radical Islam's influence on the theocratic governments of the Middle East, Africa, and Asia. But if you stay calm and smugly self-satisfied, you can easily win this argument, because duh, Christian? "No better"?

---

6 If "arguably" means "not at all, and how do gay people getting married threaten the sanctity of stuff, anyhow?" (—ed.)

Hello! The Bible makes it abundantly clear: Christianity is right (John 3:16) and Islam is wrong (Hannity 24:7).

These two faiths are nothing alike. Does this look like church to you?

Of course not. That's Mecca, under a sky blackened by pure evil, with blue-suited liberals running around among the Muslim faithful like commie Smurfs. You won't find red-staters anywhere near Mecca, unless it's an armed invasion. They won't be "making the haj" or "kissing the Kaaba" or "hijacking the jet." They know Islam is hell-bent on destroying America. Who does that sound like to you? Uh-huh. The Democratic Party, with its mullah-in-chief, Obama, bowing and scraping before Middle Eastern heads of state.[7] They're the ones turning

---

7 *Then again, Boyle, Obama also figured out where Osama bin Laden was and killed him.* (—ed.)

Guess it takes a Muslim terrorist to know one. (—RB)

Shut up, Boyle. (—ed.)

No, you shut up, editor. (—RB)

No, you. Ha-ha, I get the last word, right before we go to press. (—ed.)

America into Saudi America, or Ameristan, or the United Arab States of Amerites...OK, that's enough of that.

THE ONE TRUE CIRCUS ACT

Liberals always like to emphasize the connections between religions and cultures, because they're not comfortable with Christianity and American culture being better than everything else. They'll point out that Muslims accept Jesus as a prophet. So what? Sure, Islam has always copied off of us, stealing our best guys for their own purposes. They accept Moses, Abraham, and Jesus, but then they add Mohammad for a fourth prophet, as if Reagan didn't even count. And Rastafarians try to top us all, accepting Mohammad and adding Haile Selassie for a fifth prophet, basing their whole religious shtick on the emperor of Ethiopia, reggae music, and weed. Nice church if you can get it! Where does it all stop? There can only be one true religion, and we know ours is it, which ironically does connect us to all other fervent believers, however misplaced their erroneous faiths may be.

Real Americans reject these postmodern, "we're all spokes on the same wheel" kinds of arguments. We ARE the wheel, baby. We're the wheel and Jesus is the unicyclist, pedaling us toward salvation. Man, is he talented—he can ride a unicycle on a high wire and juggle a Bible, a Koran (or Qur'an), and a chainsaw, all at the same time, so of course Muslims accept Him as a prophet. Although we reject the liberal idea that they're just as good as we are, we do feel for people who aren't sure how to spell the name of their book of scripture. We pray for the liberation and eventual conversion of all oppressed people. We know what they're going through.

In early 2011, when Egypt's citizens erupted onto the streets like lava from volcanoes, which cause global warming way more than people do, Real Americans everywhere could sympathize. Yeah, we said, we know what it's like to chafe under the yoke of an oppressive Muslim dictator. The only difference between Mubarak and Obama is that Mubarak's been doing it for so long, he's actually pretty good at it, bringing stability to the region through oppression. We feel oppressed, too, but where's the stability? If we're going to have a Muslim for president, he should at least be a strongman propped up by wealthy Republicans. We're getting the worst of both worlds.

BEST OF TIMES + WORST OF TIMES = END TIMES

But let not your heart be troubled, or whatever Hannity says at the end of his program after explaining how liberals and Muslims and gays (oh my!) have ruined America. We know we're living in the end times. We've read the *Left Behind* series. Some of us have even read Tim LaHaye's "nonfiction" fantasy, *The Faith of Our Founding Fathers*, in which he says that Thomas Jefferson "had nothing to do with the founding of our nation" (which probably influenced the Texas School Board to replace Jefferson with Thomas Aquinas in their history curriculum). We know we won't have to endure this hellish national decline much longer. So much Biblical prophecy has already come true, and we believe the rest of it is just around the corner. If it's not, we can probably mandate the end of the world through a Constitutional Amendment.

It's a win-win for us, because if we're right and the prophecies are true, we'll be rapturing up to heaven any day now. If we're wrong (we're not) and we don't all un-man our cars right away, we get to keep on Tea Partying until we do. Hold fast to these beliefs, because godless liberals will always try to explain away the fulfillment of prophecy by showing how Christians have been saying for centuries that they were living in the end times. Well, they weren't, because these are the end times. Take a look.

Prophecy:

And this gospel of the kingdom will be preached in the whole world as a testimony to all nations, and then the end will come. It wouldn't hurt to have some kind of network for transmitting information. See what you can do, Lord. (Matthew 24:14)

Evangelicals have been trying to fulfill this one for a long time, taking the Good News to all nations who'll let us browbeat and recruit their citizens. Now God (not Al Gore!) has given us the Internet. Anybody, even a Chinese atheist or a Muslim hacker, can get online and download some Jesus.

☑ **Fulfilled!**

Prophecy:

> *There will be great distress, unequaled from the beginning of the world until now—and never to be equaled again. Bummer. If those days were not cut short, no one would survive, but for the sake of the elect they will be shortened.* (Matthew 24:21–22)

Obviously, the prophet Matthew is talking about the twenty-first century here. Bush did his best to shorten the end times during those first eight years, because as a Christian, he knew the apocalypse was going to work out great. He couldn't fulfill the prophecy, though, because he couldn't get all the Jews to leave and head for Israel. But now that a Muslim black guy is president, they'll probably scram any day now.

☑ **Almost Fulfilled!**

Prophecy:

> *At that time if anyone says to you, "Look, here is the Christ!" or "There he is!" do not believe it. For false Christs and false prophets will appear and perform great signs and miracles to deceive even the elect—if that were possible. See, I have told you ahead of time. Nyah-nyah.* (Matthew 24:23–25)

Yes, we're talking Obama. Great signs: he had that cool

O logo with the flag stripes, and those nice-looking "Yes We Can" and HOPE campaign signs and posters. The miracle is that he was elected. Talk about "deceiving the elect!"

☑ **Fulfilled!**

Prophecy:

> *I will sweep away everything from the face of the earth, declares the LORD. I will sweep away both man and beast; I will sweep away the birds from the sky and the fish in the sea—and the idols that cause the wicked to stumble…and stuff…a lot of sweeping to do.* (Zephaniah 1:2–3)

Now we're getting somewhere! Nothing says apocalypse like dead birds and fish, and we've been getting them in flocks and schools. On New Year's Eve 2010, some five thousand red-winged blackbirds fell from the sky over Beebe, Arkansas. A few days later, hundreds more landed in Louisiana. Then millions of fish washed ashore in Chesapeake Bay, Maryland. Millions more in Brazil and New Zealand. Then more birds plopped into Kentucky and Tennessee. And then a new season of *American Idol* began, and although we haven't sorted it all out yet, between that show and *Dancing with the Stars*, we know there will be wickedness and stumbling involved.

☑ **Fulfilled!**

And of course, if you've read Ezekiel and Daniel, which get a nice mash-up treatment in the Book of Revelation, and if you've slogged your way through the New Testament, where four different guys give you their versions of the life of Jesus, and if try to figure out what the hell (literally) is going on in the Book of Revelation, which the apostle John apparently wrote under the influence of painkillers (you'll need some, too, by the end of it), you'll probably want someone just to put you out of your misery, but no one will have any weapons, because the government will have confiscated them all. And whaddya know, you yourself will leave the following prophecy

☑ **Fulfilled!**

Prophecy:

> *And in those days shall men seek death, and shall not find it; and shall desire to die, and death shall flee from them. Yikes!* (Revelation 9:6)

It'll be horrible, and all around you the liberals who haven't been tossed into the lake of fire yet will be screaming and blaming the apocalypse on a lack of government oversight, and "*neither repented they of their murders, nor of their sorceries, nor of their fornication, nor of their theft*" (Revelation 9:21), which, if you've read Bill Clinton's and George Bush's memoirs, well, ☑ **Fulfilled!** You can explain that it had all been prophesied until you're blue (preferably red) in the face, but godless liberals won't listen. That's OK, though, because you're a righteous, God-fearing Real American, so you'll still be alive to fulfill this one.

Prophecy:

> *And I went unto the angel, and said unto him, Give me the little book. And he said unto me, Take it, and eat it up, and it shall make thy belly bitter, but it shall be in the mouth sweet as honey. And I took the little book and ate it up; and it was in my mouth sweet as honey; and as soon as I had eaten it, my belly was bitter. Dang!* (Revelation 10:8–10)

That's the little book in your hands right now. Not a big book, like the Bible or some fat American history tome, or the book to end all books, Revelation's book of life. This is just a little book to sweeten your Tea, Partiers. It's always sweet to have your beliefs confirmed, and *The Tea Party Guide* is all that and a bowl of sugar. But when it sits with you for a while, it may get a little bitter. We need that bitterness to get us off the couch and out into the streets to hoist our protest signs and let our voices be heard. We may be living in the end times, but we are still living. We have to do our best while we're here, because we'll be judged according to our works. Real Americans want to get written up in the book of life and get our passports stamped for the new heaven and the new earth, as required by the Constitution (Revelation 21:1, Article II, section 4). If our names aren't in the book of life, well, see ya in the lake of fire, suckers!

GOING OUT IN A BLAZE OF GLORY

After the big "Restoring Honor" rally in Washington, D.C., in August 2010, attended by 80,000 to 87,000 people (or, according to Fox News, 500,000 to 650,000; or, according to Michele Bachmann, 1.6 million), Glenn Beck said on his show two days later, "I believe we're approaching a last call. All aboard. I had nightmares, because I felt maybe I wasn't clear enough. The message I feel I'm supposed to give you is: *get behind the shield of God.*"

Anyone who follows Glenn Beck knows that he's an apocalyptic dude. The "War Room" segment of his recently canceled show always spun end-times scenarios like a break dancer on crack. Beck's endorsement of "Food Insurance" for the coming collapse of society has sold untold numbers of survivalist backpacks full of dehydrated beef stroganoff and lasagna (every backpack includes water and a little cookstove with fuel and matches). And it's only $199.99! Glenn's whole family is outfitted with these backpacks. If you don't think a two-week supply is enough, you can also get the big-family food cache for a year's peace of mind: 3,792 entrees for a mere $9,599! (The Becks don't need that, because they're Mormons and are already required to keep a year's supply of "storehouse" food. But what about *your* family? Are you apocalyprepared?)

At the very least, as Glenn will tell you, buy gold, because when this new socialist world order falls apart and the Beast is at the door, all you'll be able to do with that cash of yours is wipe the dehydrated lasagna from your ass. But gold, well… Glenn seems to think it makes sense, anyway.

At a "Divine Destiny" event the day before the big rally, he brought in one of his fave preachers, John Hagee, the author of *Can America Survive? 10 Signs That We Are the Terminal Generation*. Hagee is the

guy who says the Nazis were doing God's will by chasing the Jews out of Europe and back to the homeland. Hagee is the guy who says Hurricane Katrina was God's punishment for a planned gay parade in New Orleans. Just a really great guy. He took the opportunity at Glenn Beck's multi-denominational event to condemn pluralism and insist on the wrongness of all other beliefs but his—not that it matters, because, as Hagee pointed out, the Antichrist is on his way. Glenn Beck and Real American doomsayers ate this up like ice cream.

Hagee has also appeared on Beck's show to discuss the end of the world (which he says will take place within twenty years) and how to profit from it. His fabled *10 Signs* are like the Bill of Wrongs, showing how the Bible's terrifying end-times prophecy is all about us—not previous generations, who made it all about them—us. The end is nigh. If the following doesn't make you poop your pants and then buy backpacks and gold, this book doesn't know what will:

1. **Knowledge Explosion** (Daniel 12:4) God tells Daniel, *"many will run to and fro, and knowledge shall be increased."* Daniel may have expected a kind of Babylonian messenger service or Donkey Express, but this is a prophecy of the Internet. Hagee says there was no knowledge explosion from the time of Adam and Eve up until the twentieth century. But then, boom! We're in it.

2. **Rebirth of Israel** This came true in 1948. Did liberals understand what it meant? Of course not. Not even Jews did, because they read only the first five books of the Bible, missing all the crazy, cool stuff that happens later. They were happy to have a homeland, but had no idea that the rebirth of Israel was a sign of the end times.

3. **Birth of Nuclear War** (Zachariah 14:4) This is a description of flesh melting off of people while they're standing on their feet, "eyes consumed in their sockets," all the stuff that happens from a nuclear blast. It's like what happens to the Nazis in *Raiders of the Lost Ark*. Awesome.

4. **Universal Deception** This was Jesus telling his disciples not to let people fool them. But Hagee says it points to our time, right now, when nobody agrees on what's good and evil, what's right and wrong, so "we live in a fog of political correctness," and thank God for Glenn Beck cutting through the crap, like a crap-sword of truth.

5. **Famine** Well, this is why you buy your Food Insurance backpack.

6. **Pestilence** Hagee points to the bird flu on this one. He says it'll wipe out sinners.

7. **Earthquakes** Beck was quick to point out that we haven't actually seen an increase in earthquakes. But Hagee said earthquakes doubled in frequency in the twentieth century. Things looked tense for a moment, because Beck isn't used to being contradicted right there in his own echo chamber. But they moved on.

8. **Television** (Revelation 11:7–13) This part's a little dicey, with Hagee mentioning a prophecy of two guys who get killed by "The Beast" in the streets of Jerusalem. Within one hour the whole world will know about it, and only television could make that happen. The passage in the Bible says nothing of the sort, but Glenn Beck segued quickly to the news coverage of Tiananmen Square, so yeah, television.

9. **Skepticism** This is actually supposed to be the tenth sign, but apparently in all the discussion of earthquakes and TV, one of the signs went missing. This one's good enough to make up for it, though, because here's where we reinforce our beliefs by saying that any skepticism about our end-times theology proves the theology true. Beautiful, self-contained, completely nuts. John Hagee, ladies and gentlemen.

The rest of the show devolved into a discussion of the Antichrist, Iran, Ahmadinejad, Putin uniting Russia with the Islamic nations to attack Israel, and Beck getting Hagee to say that if Jesus were alive today, he'd watch Beck's TV show. (The missing tenth sign may well be the show's cancellation. Who's Jesus going to watch now, Rachel Maddow?)

If you research Hagee (which this book does NOT recommend) he'll mix and match items on his *10 Signs* list, adding some, taking some away, combining some. The idea is not to get too fixated on "proving" that we're in the end times, but just to accept the horrors of modern life as proof enough, backfilling as necessary with Biblical flotsam and jetsam. Then get ready for the rapture, because, as Hagee and other religious nutjobs remind us, the real Christians will be gone when the Antichrist shows up.

So the main thing is: be good, and you'll get out before the shit hits the fan.

RALLY 'ROUND THE CROSS

But let's go back to that "Restoring Honor" rally. It was the biggest Tea Party event to date, whatever the tally of attendees, but it was very different in tone than the usual protest. It's a great note to end our church-and-state discussion, because everyone expected it to be a bunch of political yelling. Nothing wrong with that, of course, but Glenn Beck actually made rally speakers sign an agreement not to make political speeches. He requested that attendees not bring protest signs. He wanted a religious gathering that was only political, really, because of the setting: the National Mall between the Lincoln Memorial and the Washington Monument.

The rally really did have a weirdly calm mood. The biggest entertainment, aside from a few heart-stirring warblings of God-and-country anthems, was tracking the liberal media coverage of the event. They couldn't figure out how to attack it. The best they could do was to criticize the date chosen for it, accusing Beck of trying to co-opt Martin Luther King, Jr.'s legacy. King delivered his "I Have a Dream" speech on the same date forty-seven years earlier, from the steps right behind Beck's podium.

True, Beck did happen to mention that he spent the night in the same hotel room where King put the finishing touches on his famous speech. He got King's niece to share the podium with him, and she seemed amazed (and frankly, terrified) to have so many white people listening to her speak. And in the weeks leading up to it all, Beck plugged the event by exhorting religious conservatives to join him and reclaim the legacy of civil rights, "because we're the ones who made it happen." But let's not dwell on Beck's revisionism or megalomania, and let's certainly not dwell on the race-baiting that has been his stock in trade since his early days in radio, and let's completely overlook the fact that if Martin Luther King, Jr. were alive today, Glenn Beck would condemn his lefty social justice leanings.

The real takeaway from the rally is that Beck showed the

Tea Party how "a soft answer turneth away wrath" (Proverbs something: something). In the end, the liberals who expected the National Mall to reverberate with vitriol and outrage were left only with their own. Beck also demonstrated that you can put church into state just by showing up. We don't have to rewrite the Constitution. We don't have to "take over" the government. We can just spread a nice, thick paste of piety on it. The event was a gigantic church service, and an unusually reflective moment for our movement, which admittedly mostly looks outward and yells about what it sees. This was, Beck said, about spiritual renewal. Weird. It won't sell as much dehydrated lasagna as hysteria and political pandering will, but "Restoring Honor" does stand as a strange, bold move by conservatism's reigning circus bear, the father of the modern Tea Party.

The Father of the Tea Party points to the Heavenly Father, in the back row, by the port-a-potties.

Oh, Mom spoke, too. Sarah Palin compared the crowd to the civil rights activists of 1963, apparently not understanding that the Great March on Washington was to stand up for rights that white conservatives were still denying to blacks a full century after slavery was abolished. On his rally recap show, Beck showed a photo of the mother of Real America in hot, fervent prayer, calling it "the most beautiful picture of Sarah Palin ever taken," as he adjusted his crotch under the desk.

Then it was back to business. Since the rally, both Beck and Palin have made headlines with inflammatory statements and bungling PR moves that in a more rigorous era would probably have ended their careers (Beck is now getting career counseling from the Heavenly Father). And that's fine. We all make mistakes, we're all sinners, but we have the capacity to transcend our stupidity. We know now that there's a spiritual foundation to the house that hosts our Tea Parties.

We've got our anger, we've still got our guns, we've still got our sense of being right, right, right, in an America that's gone wrong, wrong, wrong. But we've also got God. We've got common sense (not to be confused with *Common Sense* by Thomas Paine, who hated religion and should be shitcanned into the same non-founder dustbin as that Bible-snipper, Thomas Jefferson). And we've got each other. We know who we are, or at least who we aren't. We know what we stand for, or at least what we stand against.

In the end, the founders' spiritual counsel might be the

same advice our modern Tea Party leaders have to offer: trust your heart. Your head has never really been of much use. As the old hymn says, "'Tis a gift to be simple." And that's the answer, finally, to the question posed in the introduction to this book: *How can we tell who the Real Americans are?* Look for the simple people. The ones following their hearts and Sarah's tweets. The simple people who don't need to complicate the facts they get from talk radio or Fox News with fact-checking, who *know* what's right without thinking, who would really rather shoot than argue. It's the simple people who are going to take back this country. They're going to free it from tyranny, high taxes, low morals, and bad things. They're going to triumph over socialism.

Now, if they could just spell it.

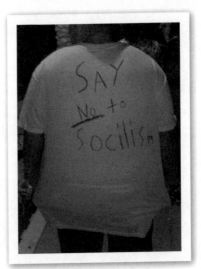

The circumstances of the world are continually changing, and the opinions of man change also; and as government is for the living, and not for the dead, it is the living only that has any right in it.

—Thomas Paine

Shake off all the fears of servile prejudices, under which weak minds are servilely crouched. Fix reason firmly in her seat, and call on her tribunal for every fact, every opinion. Question with boldness even the existence of a God; because if there be one he must more approve of the homage of reason than that of blindfolded fear.

—Thomas Jefferson

I think it's about being clever and wise.

—Thomas the Tank Engine

AFTERWORD

An Open Letter from Lobo Palin

DEAR TEABAGGERS,

Hi. I'm Lobo, one of Todd and Sarah Palin's adorable kids. Well, I'm one of Sarah's adorable kids, and Todd grudgingly lets me live. You didn't see me during the 2008 election, because Mom had enough on her plate with Bristol and Levi and learning that Africa isn't just one country. I didn't attend the convention or go on the campaign trail. I stayed in Wasilla and answered Mom's fan mail.

I'm used to it. I get hidden away a lot, stuck out back with the sled dogs, Photoshopped out of press release pictures, all that. I'm not the go-to photo-op kid for parents in the public eye. And as the principles in this book explain, kids exist to serve their parents as well as their country. So I've lived on the down-low. Until now.

Mom thinks it's time the rest of the nation caught up to Alaska in tolerance and wildlife management. Alaskans know that sometimes a child is born of the interbreeding of wolf and human. Usually, it's from some meth-addled roughneck having his way with a she-wolf. But I'm the rare wolf-child born of a human mother. And what a mother she is. Thanks to her, I'm the first wolf-child Teabagger.

Mom is tough, charming, and fertile. And I don't care how it looks in the liberal mainstream media; she is actually literate. In fact, she was originally asked to write the letter for this Afterword, because her family values are so awesome and she's so inspiring to the Tea Party movement. And she uses the principles in this book to raise me, Track, Bristol, Willow, Piper, Trig, Truck, Crunk, and Alopex Lugopus. You probably haven't heard of those last three. Don't ask.

When she told *me* to write the letter, I said, "Mom, you're on record that bestiality is an abomination, like homosexuality and estate taxes. If people find out about me, it could end your political career. They might even cancel your show." She said, "Lobo, when I tell you to write a letter, the only thing I want to hear out of you is the sound of your claws on that keyboard." So I put my tail in the chair and began to write.

I write with a sense of urgency. The principles in this book can save America. I know, because they saved me. My existence was pretty awkward for a family in politics. They could've nipped me in the bud. My mom, a woman who can take down wolves from an airplane, bring home the moose bacon, and fry it up in a pan, could have used a coat hanger or maybe faith healing to get rid of me, or drowned me in the Yukon River, as a certain reluctant adoptive father keeps suggesting.

But no. Mom took responsibility (see Growing-Up-Extremely-Right Principle #4) for her wild night in the Alaskan forest. She's raised me with the same maternal love and bossiness she lavishes on all her children, especially a certain daughter whose antics have my folks threatening her with female circumcision (Principle #7). Then again, that's illegal, and Teabaggers pay great lip service to the rule of law (Principle #5). Then again, Mom taught me to "embrace contradiction" (Principle #9). And I revere her too much to joke about how she'll embrace anything that includes "dic."

But enough about us. This is about you. It's about the future. It's about rebuilding this country from the ruin wrought by a Democratic Congress starting in 2006 and a foreign fascist sullying the presidency since 2008. Everything was fine until then! Oh, we'd run up a little debt, had a few wars going, we'd stepped on some international toes, the EPA had been gutted, government scientists were being censored, financial speculators were shaking down the poor and middle-class, New Orleans was under water, President Bush's oil and gas cronies were running amok with corrupt government agencies, and Vice President Cheney was shooting people in the face…yet, despite all this progress, the liberal left managed to wreck everything.

But we can come back. America's best days are still ahead of us. They may be way up high where we can't seem to reach them, like that shelf for my dad's "special magazines." But if my parents have taught me anything, it's that we can fail upwards. We can raise a new generation of Teabaggers. We can build that shining city on a hill, and I can't wait to chase squirrels down the streets of that city, and sit on that hill and howl my brains out.

With the help of reactionary parents, separation-of-church-and-state-defying ministers and teachers, and the right rhetoric from far-right pundits, we can bring America back from the brink of collapse. The principles you learned in this book can help us do it. How? One child at a time, that's how. One God-fearing, patriotic, browbeaten child at a time.

I'm living proof that it works. If I hadn't been raised right, you know I'd have eaten Trig by now. That cute little dude looks delicious.

—Lobo Palin

INDEX

P

ABOUT THE AUTHOR

Roland Boyle, known in impolite circles as the Tea Bastard, was born in the back seat of a bald eagle on the fourth of July in the middle of a firing range, raised by missionaries, and educated on the mean streets of Independence, Missouri. As the creator of teabastard.com, he crisscrossed the broad face of this great land, researching the new conservative movement, holding prayer meetings in public buildings, and drinking heavily. This book is the result.